Jesus Gnosis

Ulysses, Dionysus, Baal, and Lucifer

Also by Thomas Ragland (Gnostic Tom):

2003   The Noble Eightfold Path of Christ: Jesus Teaches the Dharma of Buddhism (1412000130)

2005   Buddha Turns the Kabbalah Wheel: Jewish Buddhist Resonance from a Christian Gnostic Perspective (1412064619)

2009   Jesus Gnosis Story of Simon by Philip (1426913655)

2013   Sermon on the Mount by Jesus (0989251101)

Cover design by Jude Atman

Jesus Gnosis
  Ulysses, Dionysus, Baal, and Lucifer

Thomas Ragland (Gnostic Tom)

Thomas Ragland
2015

First Printing: 2015

ISBN-13: 978-0-9892511-1-2

ISBN-10: 098925111X

Thomas Ragland
Nashville, Tennessee

Dedication

This book is dedicated to those who spend a great deal of imagination and time and effort seeking out those inverted, dynamics shifted, zoom lenses that provide for those cherished little aha moments of Gnosis. This includes the wonderful friend requested internet connections from the old days of listserv through Yahoo Groups to Facebook and beyond.

Contents

Acknowledgements

Music: Beatles, Grateful Dead, Black Sabbath, Led Zeppelin, metal. Science Fiction: Star Trek, Doctor Who. Disney: fairy tales, epic stories with values played out outside of the scope of religion, Wonderland and Neverland. My aunt's library: Harvard Classics with texts on Dionysus and Buddha, poetry by Gibran. Book stores before the internet killed them off: Nag Hammadi Library (especially the Gospel of Thomas), Buddhist scriptures, Crowley, Regardie, Fortune, and Kabbalah, magic. The Internet for supplying other curious minds to bounce ideas off of and to learn from the wonderful diversity of ways of thinking on this planet, and to acquire texts that the book stores never knew about, and search engines to fuel quests for understanding how the pieces fit.

Foreword

The Southern Baptist Church with its sacred text, the King James Bible, performed its ritual of baptism on me when I was nine years old. Someone said, "Once saved, always saved" and that it left an indelible mark on my soul. It sounded like a good deal at the time. I do think if there is a "Satan" that it is in the worldly ideas and ideals that the good folk of the small Southern town church did not, and perhaps could not, appreciate. The world was at war to fight the godless Communists, and then there were the hippies with talks about peace and love and harmony in spite of differences. There was a feminist movement to counter the oppression and discrimination against women. There was an outcry against trapping people in prisons simply for the crime of possessing drugs, little bags of plant leaves. There was a civil rights movement to counter the bigotry and injustices against the blacks. There was an ecological movement to stand up for nature against the polluting corporations. None of these seemingly good values and calls for changes were being heralded by the churches, in fact, they were being opposed by the churches. Dare I think outside their box? Dare I question their intolerance of different? Would I thereby fall from grace, become a backslider heretic?

Preface

There is only one correct answer, one correct tradition, one correct concept. This is the faith of a great deal of people, people different from each other, but agreeing on this one idea. The whole world of people is somehow lost, believing wrong, thinking wrong, acting wrong, valuing wrong, except for the select group of the chosen few. It is the sacred duty of the chosen few to point out to the rest of the world just how lost it is. It is the sacred duty of the chosen few to ensure the safety of their little oasis of truth in the desert world of "lostness", and if this means using violence against the lost savage pagans to ensure the survival of and the destiny of the chosen people in their promised land, then that is but a temporary price to pay. Faith that they have selected correctly means faith that the powers that be will be on their side and they will eventually win and be justified for and even praised for their brave crusades against evil.

Ancient Judaism invented the formula of only their god was the true god and the rest of the world was wrong, that their people is the chosen people, their land the promised land, their prophecies for their Messianic Age to come when they rule the world in the peace of the defeat of the lost world that could opposed them is a prophecy just for themselves. It was such a powerful formula of faith, the Christians took it and ran with it, taking over Europe and the Americas. It was such a powerful formula of faith, Muhammad identified with the inherited chain of prophets going back to the original Jewish idea that their god was the true god and the rest of the world was wrong, that the rest of the infidel world was confused and corrupted by Iblis (Satan). This one lens that we look though, Jews, Christians, and Muslims alike, paints in very bold strokes definite lines that divide good and evil, right and wrong, saved and damned, heaven and hell, God and Satan. The world is full of books that look through that lens – this is not one of them.

Matthew 7:15-20 Beware of false prophets, which come to you in sheep's clothing, but inwardly they are ravening wolves. Ye shall know them by their fruits. Do men gather grapes of thorns, or figs of thistles? Even so every good tree bringeth forth good fruit; but a corrupt tree bringeth forth evil fruit. A good tree cannot bring forth evil fruit, neither can a corrupt tree bring forth good fruit. Every tree that bringeth not forth good fruit is hewn down, and cast into the fire. Wherefore by their fruits ye shall know them.

Did you ever go to get your eyes tested and got new glasses and the world looked like a different place? You could then see individual leaves on the trees, birds flying in the distance, details that you couldn't see before without your new lenses. This is like that, looking at what should have been obvious, should have jumped out before. Like observing the difference between healthy bountiful fruit and twisted thorny depravity. What was Jesus talking about? What if you picked your spiritual food, your religion, in the same discerning way you picked which piece of fruit you want to eat? What if you picked who supplied you with your spiritual food, your religion, in the same discerning way you selected which market had the best and freshest selection?

So little time, so much to unlearn, to un-become, to un-identify with. Well, let's get started.

The problem with looking through only one lens is that you think it holds a monopoly on truth (Luke 11:52). You cherish that lens like an idol, but that lens doesn't show you everything. It keeps you from seeing many of the details and forbids you to look through the lenses of others that could reveal new insights.

The one lens has you being censored. There are thoughts they want to protect you from thinking. What you search for, what you resonate as truth for you, what you think about things, like yourself and God, and how everything connects and fits, all being censored by that one lens they supplied you with.

Pistis Sophia 114   Amen, amen, I say unto you: Not only will I reveal unto you all things on which ye shall question me, but from now on I will reveal unto you other things on which ye have not thought to question, which have not entered into the heart of man, and which also all the gods, who are below man, know not.

Thomas 17   Jesus said, "I shall give you what no eye has seen and what no ear has heard and what no hand has touched and what has never occurred to the human mind."

The following are lenses through which we can look at the Jesus of the Gospel. Through the "normal lens" that most modern Christians look through, some of these other lenses are shocking heresies. Imagine, if you will, a great picture that can't be seen in its entirety by just looking at it. You have to stand back and take in the whole, then get up close and examine various intricate details. Parts of it only glow under a black light. Parts of it are painted in tints that only jump out at you when you look through a special lens

Ever look through a lens that makes everything look upside down? This is one of those. The first become last, the last become first, those on top are on the bottom, and those on the bottom are now on top.

Romans Lenses

From a Roman perspective, the Jewish Zealot violence and Messianic hopes for a war hero Messiah was a problem for the Empire. The radical terrorists had taken over Jerusalem in the year 66 and it took legions of soldiers to finally defeat them and destroy the temple in 70. Then in 135 Hadrian had to recapture Jerusalem from the Messiah Simon bar Kokhba, exiling all Jews from the city and setting up temples for Jupiter and Venus.

There was a need for an anti-Messiah, a great hero that stood up against the Jewish Zealot violence and redefined Messianic hopes as being for a world of peace and love and harmony. This anti-Messiah needed to be cosmopolitan. His kingdom needed to be not of this world, seated on a spiritual landscape of mind and dreams and wisdom.

Euripides and Homer give us Dionysus and Ulysses, two strong characters that found themselves strangers in their own lands. What if this anti-Messiah was likewise a stranger? He was rejected and put on trial, like Dionysus. He was an outsider, overcome by those who had invaded his home, by those who controlled everything that rightfully belonged to him, like Ulysses. This is the story that the Roman lens would tell.

Jewish scripture mining quickly reveals that the mainstream Jerusalem Temple cult stood for xenophobia, for revolutionary violence to any outsiders, such as the Romans. A sub-thread was discovered, the persistent counter-culture world of Baal and Asherah, linked to the famous wise king Solomon, to the Samaritans, and to the hill of the Mount of Olives overlooking the Jerusalem occupied by the Temple cult. What if a new hero arrived, a great one like Dionysus or Ulysses returned to reclaim the rightful position and explain the unknown truth? What if it presented itself as a revival of the old religion, of Baal and Asherah, of feasting and music, community and sharing, healing and comforting? What if this new spirituality took the place of the Jewish Zealot Messianic dreams for revolution against the Roman Empire? What if this new religion even painted Rome as the new sacred center of itself instead of Jerusalem?

Ploughing Straight

Homer: Odyssey 18 Or if you will plough against me, let us each take a yoke of tawny oxen, well-mated and of great strength and endurance: turn me into a four acre field, and see whether you or I can drive the straighter furrow.

Luke 9:62 And Jesus said unto him, No man, having put his hand to the plough, and looking back, is fit for the kingdom of God.

The Odyssey

No ancient tale of ship and storm and hero can fail to remind some of the Odyssey chapter 10 by Homer. With enough imagination the Cyclops (Odyssey 9) is the demoniac of Gadarenes (Mark 5:1). Such well received literature could well have influenced the story telling of the Gospel.

Homer: Odyssey 9 Then Jove raised the North wind against us till it blew a hurricane, so that land and sky were hidden in thick clouds, and night sprang forth out of the heavens. We let the ships run before the gale, but the force of the wind tore our sails to tatters, so we took them down for fear of shipwreck, and rowed our hardest towards the land.

AL ISRA 17:66-67 The Lord saves from ship wreck. This idea is woven into a discussion about Iblis (Satan) trying to stir up storms of human conflict, violence and greed.

Mark 4:36-41 And when they had sent away the multitude, they took him even as he was in the ship. And there were also with him other little ships. And there arose a great storm of wind, and the waves beat into the ship, so that it was now full. And he was in the hinder part of the ship, asleep on a pillow: and they awake him, and say unto him, Master, carest thou not that we perish? And he arose, and rebuked the wind, and said unto the sea, Peace, be still. And the wind ceased, and there was a great calm. And he said unto them, Why are ye so fearful? How is it that ye have no faith? And they feared exceedingly, and said one to another, What manner of man is this, that even the wind and the sea obey him?

The ship in a storm theme links the Odyssey here with the story in Mark. The difference is that while Ulysses was a powerless mortal, Jesus was a powerful God in the same situation.

One scene from Homer's The Illiad chapter 24 comes to mind. King Priam is on a journey when he is aided by Hermes (Mercury) who puts golden flying sandals on his feet. These sandals cause King Priam to fly over the top of the sea and land to reach his destination. The difference in the Jesus story is that there is no mention of any help from a god or angel to cause him to not sink into the sea. Jesus was the one with the god powers who could bestow them to those around him at will.

Matthew 14:29 And he said, Come. And when Peter was come down out of the ship, he walked on the water, to go to Jesus.

Monster

Homer: Odyssey 9 "We sailed hence, always in much distress, till we came to the land of the lawless and inhuman Cyclopes. Now the Cyclopes neither plant nor plough, but trust in providence, and live on such wheat, barley, and grapes as grow wild without any kind of tillage, and their wild grapes yield them wine as the sun and the rain may grow them. They have no laws nor assemblies of the people, but live in caves on the tops of high mountains; each is lord and master in his family, and they take no account of their neighbours.

Homer: Odyssey 9 This was the abode of a huge monster who was then away from home shepherding his flocks. He would have nothing to do with other people, but led the life of an outlaw. He was a horrid creature, not like a human being at all, but resembling rather some crag that stands out boldly against the sky on the top of a high mountain.

Like Ulysses, Jesus faces a monster, a man so wild and strong he could not be held with chains and he lived in a cave. Unlike Ulysses, instead of outsmarting and blinding the monster, Jesus heals and rehabilitates the wild man.

Homer: Odyssey 9 "I told my men to draw the ship ashore, and stay where they were, all but the twelve best among them, who were to go along with myself.

As Ulysses took twelve, so Jesus takes his twelve apostles.

Homer: Odyssey 9 We should never be able to shift the stone which the monster had put in front of the door.

An interesting note about a stone blocking the opening of a cave that could not be moved except by super-human strength.

Homer: Odyssey 10 "They called her and she came down, unfastened the door, and bade them enter. They, thinking no evil, followed her, all except Eurylochus, who suspected mischief and stayed outside. When she had got them into her house, she set them upon benches and seats and mixed them a mess with cheese, honey, meal, and pramnian but she drugged it with wicked poisons to make them forget their homes, and when they had drunk she turned them into pigs by a stroke of her wand, and shut them up in her pigsties. They were like pigs—head, hair, and all, and they grunted just as pigs do; but their senses were the same as before, and they remembered everything.

In the Ulysses story, it was his sailing companions that were turned into pigs, the twelve minus the one who had deserted them. Jesus proved more powerful and made pigs out of the exorcized demons.

Mark 5:1-13 And they came over unto the other side of the sea, into the country of the Gadarenes. And when he was come out of the ship, immediately there met him out of the tombs a man with an unclean spirit, Who had his dwelling among the tombs; and no man could bind him, no, not with chains: Because that he had been often bound with fetters and chains, and the chains had been plucked asunder by him, and the fetters broken in pieces: neither could any man tame him. And always, night and day, he was in the mountains, and in the tombs, crying, and cutting himself with stones. But when he saw Jesus afar off, he ran and worshipped him, And cried with a loud voice, and said, What have I to do with thee, Jesus, thou Son of the most high God? I adjure thee by God, that thou torment me not. For he said unto him, Come out of the man, thou unclean spirit. And he asked him, What is thy name? And he answered, saying, My name is Legion: for we are many. And he besought him much that he would not send them away out of the country. Now there was there nigh unto the mountains a great herd of swine feeding. And all the devils besought him, saying, Send us into the swine, that we may enter into them. And forthwith Jesus gave them leave. And the unclean spirits went out, and entered into the swine: and the herd ran violently down a steep place into the sea, (they were about two thousand;) and were choked in the sea.

Tree

Homer: Odyssey 7 Outside the gate of the outer court there is a large garden of about four acres with a wall all round it. It is full of beautiful trees – pears, pomegranates, and the most delicious apples. There are luscious figs also, and olives in full growth. The fruits never rot nor fail all the year round, neither winter nor summer, for the air is so soft that a new crop ripens before the old has dropped.

Five types of trees are listed: pears, pomegranates, apples, figs, and olives. I wonder if these are the five trees referenced in Thomas 19.

Thomas 19 Jesus said, "Blessed is he who came into being before he came into being. If you become my disciples and listen to my words, these stones will minister to you. For there are five trees for you in Paradise which remain undisturbed summer and winter and whose leaves do not fall. Whoever becomes acquainted with them will not experience death."

When life does not automatically provide fruit, something is wrong. In sync with God, fruit falls automatically as you become hungry. In sync with God, mountains should move out of your way.

The expectation of unfailing fruit is not too much to ask by a god, or even by one visiting a god. It is in a Greek poetic sense that the disappointment of Jesus regarding the lack of figs is made clear. Where is the fruitfulness that is evidence of God being present in his holy place? There is no fruit. There is no God present. Jerusalem is a failure at being the garden home of God. If God lived there, there would be fruit, but there is not. Violence and division and fear abound, but where is the spiritual fruit?

Mark 11:12-14 And on the morrow, when they were come from Bethany, he was hungry: And seeing a fig tree afar off having leaves, he came, if haply he might find any thing thereon: and when he came to it, he found nothing but leaves; for the time of figs was not yet. And Jesus answered and said unto it, No man eat fruit of thee hereafter for ever. And his disciples heard it.

If Jerusalem won't feed me, let it only poison the world from here on out.

Mark 11:20-24 And in the morning, as they passed by, they saw the fig tree dried up from the roots. And Peter calling to remembrance saith unto him, Master, behold, the fig tree which thou cursedst is withered away. And Jesus answering saith unto them, Have faith in God. For verily I say unto you, That whosoever shall say unto this mountain, Be thou removed, and be thou cast into the sea; and shall not doubt in his heart, but shall believe that those things which he saith shall come to pass; he shall have whatsoever he saith. Therefore I say unto you, What things soever ye desire, when ye pray, believe that ye receive them, and ye shall have them.

Synergy with the True God, above and beyond Jerusalem's fruitless tree. This is symbolic. This is a parable, not a documentary.

Carpenter

Homer: Odyssey 23　Then I cut off the top boughs of the olive tree and left the stump standing. This I dressed roughly from the root upwards and then worked with carpenter's tools well and skilfully, straightening my work by drawing a line on the wood, and making it into a bed-prop.

For all of the allusions to Ulysses in the gospels, it may be added that Ulysses was also a carpenter. Matthew 13:55 identifies Jesus as "the carpenter's son" while Mark makes Jesus to himself be identified as "the carpenter" with no mention of Joseph. The words "the carpenter" are omitted in some versions of Mark 6:3. So many variations of the same story is a clue that deliberate changes are in play, changes on purpose, changes with an agenda, to reference something known, something that needed to be linked to, needed to be referenced for those who have ears to hear.

Vanishing

Homer: Odyssey 7　Presently Ulysses got up to go towards the town; and Minerva shed a thick mist all round him to hide him in case any of the proud Phaeacians who met him should be rude to him, or ask him who he was. Then, as he was just entering the town, she came towards him in the likeness of a little girl carrying a pitcher. She stood right in front of him.... On this she led the way, and Ulysses followed in her steps; but not one of the Phaeacians could see him as he passed through the city in the midst of them; for the great goddess Minerva in her good will towards him had hidden him in a thick cloud of darkness.

An interesting resonance with Ulysses in that the goddess Minerva, who followed and protected him like the Holy Spirit in the life of Jesus, conjured up a fog to hide him from the crowds who may be hostile to him as a then poor stranger. Also note the little girl carrying a pitcher to show him the way, reminding us of the man carrying the pitcher showing the way to the upper room on the gospel story (Mark 14:13).

Homer: Odyssey 10 She passed through the midst of us without our knowing it, for who can see the comings and goings of a god, if the god does not wish to be seen?

John 10:39-42 Therefore they sought again to take him: but he escaped out of their hand, and went away again beyond Jordan into the place where John at first baptized; and there he abode. And many resorted unto him, and said, John did no miracle: but all things that John spake of this man were true. And many believed on him there.

Luke 4:28-30 And all they in the synagogue, when they heard these things, were filled with wrath, And rose up, and thrust him out of the city, and led him unto the brow of the hill whereon their city was built, that they might cast him down headlong. But he passing through the midst of them went his way,

The walking right through a large hostile crowd could be interpreted as a Docetist view of Jesus as only appearing to be really human. The walking through walls, walking on water, appearing out of nowhere and disappearing imply that Jesus was not a normal tangible human. He was a magical wizard or an avatar of a god or something else quite beyond normal, or like Ulysses, he had a direction connection to the synergy of powerful magic.

John 20:26 And after eight days again his disciples were within, and Thomas with them: then came Jesus, the doors being shut, and stood in the midst, and said, Peace be unto you.

Return

Homer: Odyssey 16 If you see them ill-treating me, steel your heart against my sufferings; even though they drag me feet foremost out of the house, or throw things at me, look on and do nothing beyond gently trying to make them behave more reasonably; but they will not listen to you, for the day of their reckoning is at hand.

Just as the intruders were determined to kill Ulysses and take control of his house once and for all, in the Gospel story the self-imposed leaders of Judaism were determined to kill Jesus and maintain control of the Temple. In each story the last became first and the first became last. And just like once Ulysses had murdered the intruders and had to then abandon his home, so once the leaders of the Jewish revolt were silenced in the year 70, the Temple had to be abandoned in total destruction. As Minerva leaves Ulysses with the thought of peace after all that had happened, so too the Holy Spirit leaves Jesus with a sense of peace and control beyond the touches of the physical world with its battles and buildings and politics. It is classic Greek tragedy at play here.

Homer: Odyssey 16 "Ulysses, noble son of Laertes, it is now time for you to tell your son: do not keep him in the dark any longer, but lay your plans for the destruction of the suitors, and then make for the town. I will not be long in joining you, for I too am eager for the fray." As she spoke she touched him with her golden wand. First she threw a fair clean shirt and cloak about his shoulders; then she made him younger and of more imposing presence; she gave him back his colour, filled out his cheeks, and let his beard become dark again. Then she went away and Ulysses came back inside the hut. His son was astounded when he saw him, and turned his eyes away for fear he might be looking upon a god.

This is the goddess Minerva speaking to Ulysses, preparing him to gain the strength to retake his home from the intruders that had taken over while he was away. His transformation is a visible transfiguration. He looked like a god. The position of Minerva in the Odyssey is like the Holy Spirit in the gospels. The story of the home-owner being away and the people living in his house disrespecting him and then plotting to kill his son is a major theme in the Odyssey by Homer. Odysseus is away on a journey, thought to be dead, while suitors are in his home trying to convince Penelope his wife to marry one of them instead. They plot to kill Telemachus his son in order to take full control of his estate. Ulysses has finally returned in the climax of the story.

Thomas 65 He said, "There was a good man who owned a vineyard. He leased it to tenant farmers so that they might work it and he might collect the produce from them. He sent his servant so that the tenants might give him the produce of the vineyard. They seized his servant and beat him, all but killing him. The servant went back and told his master. The master said, 'Perhaps he did not recognize them.' He sent another servant. The tenants beat this one as well. Then the owner sent his son and said, 'Perhaps they will show respect to my son.' Because the tenants knew that it was he who was the heir to the vineyard, they seized him and killed him. Let him who has ears hear."

Thomas 66 Jesus said, "Show me the stone which the builders have rejected. That one is the cornerstone."

Solomon's Jerusalem lasted for that frozen moment, like a Camelot, like an El Dorado, like a Shangri La. His wisdom was rejected, his gardens torn down, his monuments destroyed. Solomon in spirit lay in exile from the Palestinian world until Jesus appeared to represent the return. Jesus represented the son of David, Solomon, the wisest man who ever lived, the fabled magician, the herald of Baal.

Homer: Odyssey 22 When she saw all the corpses and such a quantity of blood, she was beginning to cry out for joy, for she saw that a great deed had been done; but Ulysses checked her, "Old woman," said he, "rejoice in silence; restrain yourself, and do not make any noise about it; it is an unholy thing to vaunt over dead men. Heaven's doom and their own evil deeds have brought these men to destruction, for they respected no man in the whole world, neither rich nor poor, who came near them, and they have come to a bad end as a punishment for their wickedness and folly.

Mark 13:26 And then shall they see the Son of man coming in the clouds with great power and glory.

Poetic justice. Instant karma. Zealots defeated. Jerusalem broken.

Homer: Odyssey 16 A father could not be more delighted at the return of an only son, the child of his old age, after ten years' absence in a foreign country and after having gone through much hardship. He embraced him, kissed him all over as though he had come back from the dead, and spoke fondly to him saying: "So you are come, Telemachus, light of my eyes that you are. When I heard you had gone to Pylos I made sure I was never going to see you any more. Come in, my dear child, and sit down, that I may have a good look at you now you are home again; I wish I were as young as you are and in my present mind; if I were son to Ulysses, or, indeed, Ulysses himself, I would rather some one came and cut my head off, but I would go to the house and be the bane of every one of these men. If they were too many for me – I being single handed – I would rather die fighting in my own house than see such disgraceful sights day after day, strangers grossly maltreated, and men dragging the women servants about the house in an unseemly way, wine drawn recklessly, and bread wasted all to no purpose for an end that shall never be accomplished." Jove has made us a race of only sons. Laertes was the only son of Arceisius, and Ulysses only son of Laertes. I am myself the only son of Ulysses who left me behind him when he went away, so that I have never been of any use to him. Hence it comes that my house is in the hands of numberless marauders;

The scene is where Ulysses sees his son Telemachus for the first time in years. That the "son" should return to "the house" and do something about the situation there is of note. It is also a curiosity that Telemachus is the "only son" of Ulysses. We see a thread weaving through the father finding the lost son (Luke 15:24) and the vineyard parable of the master sending his son to take back control of the wine (Thomas 65). The intruders of the vineyard plotted to kill the son (Mark 12:6-8), the master's only son. What will the owner do when he comes, asks Mark 12:9? If this is an allusion to the Odyssey story, the answer is the same thing that Ulysses did when he returned home. It fits the story of the destruction of the priesthood and the temple, but it was not at the return of "Jesus the rejected", it was rather at the coming of Titus, the only son of Vespasian.

Homer: Odyssey 18 Nay, he will be here soon; may heaven send you home quietly first that you may not meet with him in the day of his coming, for once he is here the suitors and he will not part bloodlessly."

Mark 12:1-9 What shall therefore the lord of the vineyard do? He will come and destroy the husbandmen, and will give the vineyard unto others. And have ye not read this scripture; The stone which the builders rejected is become the head of the corner: This was the Lord's doing, and it is marvellous in our eyes?

Blind

Plato's Timaeus contains a discussion about the sense of sight. In the story Timaeus learns from Socrates the secrets of the origin of the universe. Socrates was to be executed for his philosophy. Homer's

Odyssey, book 11, has a blind man in Hades called Tiresias recognize Ulysses even though he was blind. The duality of the disciples who could see Jesus not understanding him and this blind man who saw him more clearly than anyone is an important theme in Mark.

Nicodemus 5:20-23   Then another certain Jew came forth, and said, I was blind, could hear sounds, but could not see any one; and as Jesus was going along, I heard the multitude passing by, and I asked what was there? They told me that Jesus was passing by: then I cried out, saying, Jesus, Son of David, have mercy on me. And he stood still, and commanded that I should be brought to him, and said to me, What wilt thou? I said, Lord that I may receive my sight. He said to me, Receive thy sight: and presently I saw, and followed him, rejoicing and giving thanks.

Mark 10:46-52 And they came to Jericho: and as he went out of Jericho with his disciples and a great number of people, blind Bartimaeus, the son of Timaeus, sat by the highway side begging. And when he heard that it was Jesus the Nazarite, he began to cry out, and say, Jesus, thou son of David, have mercy on me. And many charged him that he should hold his peace: but he cried the more a great deal, Thou son of David, have mercy on me. And Jesus stood still, and commanded him to be called. And they call the blind man, saying unto him, Be of good comfort, rise; he calleth thee. And he, casting away his garment, rose, and came to Jesus. And Jesus answered and said unto him, What wilt thou that I should do unto thee? The blind man said unto him, Lord, that I might receive my sight. And Jesus said unto him, Go thy way; thy faith hath made thee whole. And immediately he received his sight, and followed Jesus in the way.

Ship

Homer: Odyssey 2   Then Minerva bethought her of another matter. She took his shape, and went round the town to each one of the crew, telling them to meet at the ship by sundown. She went also to Noemon son of Phronius, and asked him to let her have a ship – which he was very ready to do.

It is an interesting parallel to the Odyssey that having access to ships is a major theme in the gospel of Jesus. As the goddess Minerva rounds up the crew for Ulysses, the Holy Spirit inspires a crew for Jesus. Mark 4:36 portrays Jesus as having a fleet of boats. He teaches from a boat, stills storms from a boat, walks on the water to a boat, appears and disappears in various towns by means of a boat. The boat and storm theme carries over into the tradition where it is Paul that is shipwrecked on a sea voyage to Rome (2 Corinthians 11:25).

Mountain

Homer: Odyssey 6   When she had said this Minerva went away to Olympus, which they say is the everlasting home of the gods. Here no wind beats roughly, and neither rain nor snow can fall; but it abides in everlasting sunshine and in a great peacefulness of light, wherein the blessed gods are illumined for ever and ever. This was the place to which the goddess went when she had given instructions to the girl.

Minerva in the Odyssey serves as a companion "Holy Spirit" intercessor and synchronizer for Ulysses. The ascension into Olympus and the idea of the "heaven" of Olympus reminds us of Jesus ascending into heaven. As Minerva went to Olympus to be with her father Jove, so Jesus went to heaven to be with his Father God. A Greek audience in the time at which the gospels were first being presented would not have failed to see the resonance here. A Jewish audience would have been confused, apart from the appreciating of the tales of Enoch transforming into Metatron.

Rich

Homer: Odyssey 18   Man is the vainest of all creatures that have their being upon earth. As long as heaven vouchsafes him health and strength, he thinks that he shall come to no harm hereafter, and even when the blessed gods bring sorrow upon him, he bears it as he needs must, and makes the best of it; for God Almighty gives men their daily minds day by day. I know all about it, for I was a rich man once, and did much wrong in the stubbornness of my pride, and in the confidence that my father and my brothers would support me; therefore let a man fear God in all things always, and take the good that heaven may see fit to send him without vainglory.

Thomas 63 Jesus said, "There was a rich man who had much money. He said, 'I shall put my money to use so that I may sow, reap, plant, and fill my storehouse with produce, with the result that I shall lack nothing.' Such were his intentions, but that same night he died. Let him who has ears hear."

Luke 12:16-21 And he spake a parable unto them, saying, The ground of a certain rich man brought forth plentifully: And he thought within himself, saying, What shall I do, because I have no room where to bestow my fruits? And he said, This will I do: I will pull down my barns, and build greater; and there will I bestow all my fruits and my goods. And I will say to my soul, Soul, thou hast much goods laid up for many years; take thine ease, eat, drink, and be merry. But God said unto him, Thou fool, this night thy soul shall be required of thee: then whose shall those things be, which thou hast provided? So is he that layeth up treasure for himself, and is not rich toward God.

Kindness

Homer: Odyssey 6 This is only some poor man who has lost his way, and we must be kind to him, for strangers and foreigners in distress are under Jove's protection, and will take what they can get and be thankful; so, girls, give the poor fellow something to eat and drink, and wash him in the stream at some place that is sheltered from the wind."

Jove is the "father god" in the Odyssey. The kindness to strangers and foreigners advocated by Jesus in the gospels is strangely more at home in Greek literature than in Jewish scripture.

Luke 10:29-37 But he, willing to justify himself, said unto Jesus, And who is my neighbour? And Jesus answering said, A certain man went down from Jerusalem to Jericho, and fell among thieves, which stripped him of his raiment, and wounded him, and departed, leaving him half dead. And by chance there came down a certain priest that way: and when he saw him, he passed by on the other side. And likewise a Levite, when he was at the place, came and looked on him, and passed by on the other side. But a certain Samaritan, as he journeyed, came where he was: and when he saw him, he had compassion on him, and went to him, and bound up his wounds, pouring in oil and wine, and set him on his own beast, and brought him to an inn, and took care of him. And on the morrow when he departed, he took out two pence, and gave them to the host, and said unto him, Take care of him; and whatsoever thou spendest more, when I come again, I will repay thee. Which now of these three, thinkest thou, was neighbour unto him that fell among the thieves? And he said, He that shewed mercy on him. Then said Jesus unto him, Go, and do thou likewise.

Seat

Homer: Odyssey 7 "Alcinous," said he, "it is not creditable to you that a stranger should be seen sitting among the ashes of your hearth; every one is waiting to hear what you are about to say; tell him, then, to rise and take a seat on a stool inlaid with silver, and bid your servants mix some wine and water that we may make a drink-offering to Jove the lord of thunder, who takes all well-disposed suppliants under his protection; and let the housekeeper give him some supper, of whatever there may be in the house." When Alcinous heard this he took Ulysses by the hand, raised him from the hearth, and bade him take the seat of Laodamas, who had been sitting beside him, and was his favourite son. A maid servant then brought him water in a beautiful golden ewer and poured it into a silver basin for him to wash his hands, and she drew a clean table beside him; an upper servant brought him bread and offered him many good things of what there was in the house, and Ulysses ate and drank. Then Alcinous said to one of the servants, "Pontonous, mix a cup of wine and hand it round that we may make drink-offerings to Jove the lord of thunder, who is the protector of all well-disposed suppliants."

The same theme of better and worse seats at a banquet link this passage from the Odyssey to this parable in Luke. It is of note that Jove is the "lord of thunder" and the disciples who are called the "sons of thunder" (Mark 3:17) had requested the "best seats" in the kingdom of Christ. This begs the question, is this a parable or an event?

Mark 10:37 They said unto him, Grant unto us that we may sit, one on thy right hand and the other on thy left hand in thy glory.

Luke 14:7-11 And he put forth a parable to those which were bidden, when he marked how they chose out the chief rooms; saying unto them. When thou art bidden of any man to a wedding, sit not down in the highest room; lest a more honourable man than thou be bidden of him; And he that bade thee and him come and say to thee, Give this man place; and thou begin with shame to take the lowest room. But when thou art bidden, go and sit down in the lowest room;

that when he that bade thee cometh, he may say unto thee, Friend, go up higher: then shalt thou have worship in the presence of them that sit at meat with thee. For whosoever exalteth himself shall be abased; and he that humbleth himself shall be exalted.

Fasting

In the Gospel according to the Hebrews, the following is added after Matthew 26:29

And James, his brother, says to him, "No more shall I eat bread henceforth until the day the Son of Man is raised from among those who sleep."

Homer: Odyssey 16 "I understand and heed you," replied Eumaeus; "you need instruct me no further, only I am going that way say whether I had not better let poor Laertes know that you are returned. He used to superintend the work on his farm in spite of his bitter sorrow about Ulysses, and he would eat and drink at will along with his servants; but they tell me that from the day on which you set out for Pylos he has neither eaten nor drunk as he ought to do, nor does he look after his farm, but sits weeping and wasting the flesh from off his bones."

In the Gospel according to the Hebrews, the following is added after Matthew 28:15: But the archpriests knew what had happened because of the linen cloth. Now the Lord, when he had given the linen cloth to the servant of the priest, went to James and appeared to him, for James had sworn that he would not eat bread from that hour wherein he had drunk the Lord's cup until he should see him risen again from among those who sleep. And he said to him, "Hail!" And he called to the servants, who were greatly amazed. "Bring," said the Lord, "a table and bread." He took bread and blessed and broke and gave it to James the Just and said to him, "My brother, eat your bread, for the man has risen from those who sleep."

The fasting of James until the Son of Man returns is like the fasting of Laertes until Ulysses returns. It is of note that it is Eumaeus who knows this in the Odyssey while in the gospel account it was disciples on "the road to" Emmaus who are of the first to hear that Jesus was back from Hades.

Hades

Homer: Odyssey 10 "And the goddess answered, 'Ulysses, noble son of Laertes, you shall none of you stay here any longer if you do not want to, but there is another journey which you have got to take before you can sail homewards. You must go to the house of Hades and of dread Proserpine to consult the ghost of the blind Theban (Thebes, as in the home of Dionysus) prophet Teiresias whose reason is still unshaken. To him alone has Proserpine left his understanding even in death, but the other ghosts flit about aimlessly.' "I was dismayed when I heard this. I sat up in bed and wept, and would gladly have lived no longer to see the light of the sun, but presently when I was tired of weeping and tossing myself about, I said, 'And who shall guide me upon this voyage- for the house of Hades is a port that no ship can reach.'

Part of the creed of Christianity is that Jesus descended into hell before he resurrected. In Greek mythology, hell is the house of Hades. Before Ulysses could return to reclaim his house, he had to take a side trip though Hades. It is interesting how the trip to hell and back became part of the Jesus legend. Before he could ascend into heaven, he had to descend into hell.

Trinity

Homer: Odyssey 18 Father Jove, Minerva, and Apollo

The Father (Jove), the Holy Ghost (Minerva), and the Sun god Son (Apollo) were already thought of as a Trinity in the Greek world. In the Egyptian world, father Osiris and mother Isis and baby Horus formed a Trinity. In fact the statues of mother Isis and baby Horus were adopted by the Christians and identified as mother Mary and baby Jesus.

Recognition

Homer: Odyssey 18 As soon as Euryclea had got the scarred limb in her hands and had well hold of it, she recognized it and dropped the foot at once. The leg fell into the bath, which rang out and was overturned, so that all the water was spilt on the ground; Euryclea's eyes between her joy and her grief filled with tears, and she could not speak, but she caught Ulysses by the beard and said, "My dear child, I am sure you must be Ulysses himself, only I did not know you till I had actually touched and handled you."

Euryclea recognized Ulysses by touching his scar. Thomas recognized Jesus by touching his scar (John 20:27).

Homer: Odyssey 18   Since it has been borne in upon you by heaven to recognize me, hold your tongue, and do not say a word about it to any one else in the house

The way that Ulysses tells those who know who he is to keep it a secret reminds us of the way that Jesus tells those who know who he is to keep it a secret.

Matthew 16:20   Then charged he his disciples that they should tell no man that he was Jesus the Christ.

Dionysus (Prototype)

What does the god of wine, women and song have to do with Jesus? Looking through the lens of Puritanical Christianity, it would seem to be next to nothing at all.

The Bacchae is a play written by the ancient Greek poet Euripides, discovered by and completed by his son and first performed after his death in the year 405 BC. It explores the myths of Dionysus, "the All-Father's mystic son", woven into a tragic tale of "old clashes with new", of injustice and revenge, tradition and inspiration. Euripides exposes the shortcoming of stubborn devotion and the tragic results that come of actually encountering one of the gods so imagined by poets and philosophers and weavers of religion. This became the example of how to tell a story about a god encountering people in the ancient Greek speaking world. Stories were told through dramatic plays, actors playing roles that represented aspects of the human experience. Plays were religious dramas, weaving together the mystery of initiation, the associated myths, and the spirituality of the subject. We have to consider, in what way was the Gospel originally thought of as a play? In a world where only a small percentage of people could read, the theatre was the vehicle for sharing ideas. It was the ancient equivalent of movies and television series.

Bacchae: For his kingdom, it is there, in the dancing and the prayer, in the music and the laughter, in the vanishing of care.

John 14:9 Jesus saith unto him, Have I been so long time with you, and yet hast thou not known me, Philip? He that hath seen me hath seen the Father; and how sayest thou then, Shew us the Father?

In his trial, Pentheus asks: Where is he? For mine eyes discern him not. Dionysus explains that God is: Where I am! Tis thine own impurity that veils him from thee.

The appearance of a man who is really God's son is the story of both the Bacchae and the Gospel.

Tomb

The sacred tomb of Semele, overgrown with wild vines, is the setting for the first appearance of Dionysus in the play.

John 20:1   The first day of the week cometh Mary Magdalene early, when it was yet dark, unto the sepulchre, and seeth the stone taken away from the sepulchre.

There is a reversal between the Bacchae and the Gospel. In the Bacchae, Dionysus is visiting the tomb of his mother. In the Gospel, Mary Magdalene is visiting the tomb of Jesus.

John 11:31   The Jews then which were with her in the house, and comforted her, when they saw Mary, that she rose up hastily and went out, followed her, saying, She goeth unto the grave to weep there.

Another scene from the Gospel that comes to mind is Mary at the grave of Lazarus, a person much beloved by Jesus who had recently died. In this story, Jesus brings Lazarus back to life. Dionysus, in all of his godlike powers, could not bring Semele back to life.

Lightning's Bride

Semele, a human woman, was pregnant with the son of the great god Zeus. Lightning from the sky is symbolic of the power of Zeus.

Protevangelium of James 19   And they stood in the place of the cave: and behold a bright cloud overshadowing the cave.

Matthew 1:18   Now the birth of Jesus Christ was on this wise: When as his mother Mary was espoused to Joseph, before they came together, she was found with child of the Holy Ghost.

AL 'IMRAN 3.47   She said: "O my Lord! How shall I have a son when no man hath touched me?" He said: "Even so: Allah createth what He willeth: When He hath decreed a plan, He but saith to it, 'Be,' and it is!

A child being born, just because God wills it, of a human mother who didn't become pregnant by relations with a human man is the theme of this lens.

Unsupportive Family

In the Bacchae, Semele's sisters did not believe Semele was pregnant with the child of Zeus. They mocked her and disrespected baby Dionysus. She was not revered as the sacred choice of Zeus. Dionysus was not revered as the sacred child of Zeus. This is the premise of the play that Dionysus is returned to Thebes, the place of his birth, to set the record straight.

Thomas 99 The disciples said to him, "Your brothers and your mother are standing outside." He said to them, "Those here who do the will of my father are my brothers and my mother. It is they who will enter the kingdom of my father."

There is this same sense of tension between Dionysus and his relatives in the Bacchae as between Jesus and his relatives in the Gospel. It wasn't just that outsiders to the event of a mortal woman giving birth to a "god son" had their doubts. It was this mocking rejection by those who should have been the most supportive.

Mark 3:21 And when his friends heard of it, they went out to lay hold on him: for they said, He is beside himself.

In the Gospel, the family rejection is extended to friends, and even to devoted followers.

John 6:66 From that time many of his disciples went back, and walked no more with him.

Mark 6:4 But Jesus, said unto them, a prophet is not without honour, but in his own country, and among his own kin, and in his own house.

In the Bacchae, in the opening speech by Dionysus, he explains that he had travelled all around the world teaching his dances and rites of mysteries, showing people how to see God manifest in their direct experience, and how he has returned to his home, to Thebes. After a world of acclaim and praise, he returns to rejection and scorn and even to scheming plots against him. It is in this balanced tension between the absolute truth and power of the true son of god born of a mortal woman and the frustration of not being accepted that the Gospel Jesus is introduced, just like Dionysus.

Luke 3:23 And Jesus himself began to be about thirty years of age, being (as was supposed) the son of Joseph, which was the son of Heli,

Jesus begins teaching when he was thirty years old. Where was he before? Travelling the world like young Dionysus? Exploring humanity, philosophy, and perspective, from Egypt to India? From Plato to Buddha? Suddenly reappearing, returning home, after so many years away! How to explain himself? To the religious leaders of the people? To his family and friends? He was now alien to them, an outsider, even though he should be seen as their special citizen, their famous son.

Local boy makes good, and after all this time is finally returning home with a hero's welcome. They should lay out palm branches in the street for him to walk upon. They should follow him with minstrel song, throw him a "welcome home" feast, give him a place of honor in the community, the respect he is indeed due.

Misunderstood Counter-Culture

Matthew 11:19 The Son of man came eating and drinking, and they say, Behold a man gluttonous, and a winebibber, a friend of publicans and sinners. But wisdom is justified of her children.

Bacchae: A messenger reports back: There beneath the trees sleeping they lay, like wild things flung at ease in the forest; one half sinking on a bed of deep pine greenery; one with careless head amid the fallen oak leaves; all most cold in purity – not as thy tale was told of wine-cups and wild music and the chase for love amid the forest's loneliness.

When all we know about a group of people is from the reports of those who didn't like them, didn't understand them, didn't appreciate them, then what we know is distorted through their lens. Bunch of damn hippies living in the woods, they think, imagining what that must be like from the perspective of their civilized suburban lives. People like to label things they don't understand.

Mark 7:2 And when they saw some of his disciples eat bread with defiled, that is to say, with unwashen, hands, they found fault.

Once it is agreed to divide the world between us and them, good and bad, saved and damned, the different people become judged for anything and everything. Oh, look at them, they are eating lunch without washing their hands. We can't be associated with those types! The same counter-culture difference between the followers of Dionysus and the "normal" people was also hinted at for the followers of Jesus.

Euripides shares: The world with a great wind blows. Shining, and not from thee; blowing to beautiful things, on, amid dark and light, till life, through the trammeling of laws that are not right, breaks, clean and pure, and sings glorying to God in the height!

John 1:5 And the light shineth in darkness; and the darkness comprehended it not.

The powers that be are holding back needed change. They can't understand the vision of the new god at hand. The fresh breeze blowing in, the dawning of new light, awakening and exposing the things that are not right, blows through the minds of those who can feel it and understand it and participate in it. But this is not mainstream, not common. This is all taking place in a misunderstood counter-culture. This is happening not because of the culturally accepted religion, but rather, it is happening in spite of it.

Bacchae: Avert thine eyes from the lore of the wise, that have honour in proud men's sight. The simple nameless herd of humanity hath deeds and faith that are enough for me!

Luke 6:26 Woe unto you, when all men shall speak well of you! For so did their fathers to the false prophets.

Matthew 5:5 Blessed are the meek: for they shall inherit the earth.

It is not the organized religion at hand that defines what spirituality really means. It is not the general consensus vote of the herd that defines the correct decision. It is not the battle victories of the warriors that defines who this planet really belongs to. It is not the famous that deserve to be admired. It is not the experts that will discover the next breakthrough paradigm shift.

Hera's Plot – Light Flash

In the Bacchae, the myth of the goddess Hera being jealous of the birth of Dionysus is mentioned in the dialog. The god Zeus and the goddess Hera had six children together, Ares, Hephaestus, Hebe, Eileithyia, Enyo, and Eris. When she discovered that Zeus had a son by a mortal woman, she wanted to destroy both the child and the mother.

Matthew 2:13-14 And when they were departed, behold, the angel of the Lord appeareth to Joseph in a dream, saying, Arise, and take the young child and his mother, and flee into Egypt, and be thou there until I bring thee word: for Herod will seek the young child to destroy him. When he arose, he took the young child and his mother by night, and departed into Egypt.

In the Gospel story, "Herod" fails and both mother and divine child escape. In the myth behind the Bacchae, "Hera" has tricked Zeus into appearing in his lightning form for the pregnant human mother who dies from the experience. Zeus then takes the infant into his own body and protects him until he is ready to be born a second time.

Thomas 15   Jesus said, "When you see one who was not born of woman, prostrate yourselves on your faces and worship him. That one is your Father."

This verse in the Gospel of Thomas is interesting in light of the story of Dionysus being born from the side of Zeus, for this would make this birth special since it was not being born from a woman's body. He was the twice born, the born again.

Protevangelium of James 19   And they stood in the place of the cave: and behold a bright cloud overshadowing the cave. And the midwife said: My soul is magnified this day, because mine eyes have seen marvellous things: for salvation is born unto Israel. And immediately the cloud withdrew itself out of the cave, and a great light appeared in the cave so that our eyes could not endure it. And by little and little that light withdrew itself until the young child appeared: and it went and took the breast of its mother Mary.

In the Gospel story, the great light that appeared over Mary didn't kill Mary. It served to present the birthing event of Jesus as the son of the great light.

Calling

Dionysus explains in the Bacchae: "From empty chambers the bare mountain side is made their home, and all their hearts are flame. Yea, I have bound upon the necks of them the harness of my rites."

Mark 6:46   And when he had sent them away, he departed into a mountain to pray.

Both Dionysus and Jesus lead their devotees into nature, away from civilization. The getting away from it all and living a simple life inspired the monastic orders.

Matthew 3:11 [John the Baptist:] I indeed baptize you with water unto repentance. But he that cometh after me is mightier than I, whose shoes I am not worthy to bear: he shall baptize you with the Holy Ghost, and with fire:

There are many initiation rituals for spiritual groups going back to as long as there has been the desire to connect to a larger movement in order to individually advance. The being immersed into

conformity is the way of John in the Gospel and Pentheus in the Bacchae, each of which loses their head in the end. John can't walk in the
shoes of the new god. Pentheus can't disguise himself as a devotee to
the new god. There is a sense of real Gnosis at play in both stories.
The burning fire in the heart is passion, direct connection, personal
transformation, not just a membership card in being one of the many.

Thomas 90 Jesus said, "Come unto me, for my yoke is easy and
my lordship is mild, and you will find repose for yourselves."

Interesting that the concept of putting on a harness or yoke is
common to both being initiated in the following of Dionysus and of
Jesus. There is a direct connection between the new god and the devotee. In both stories, the initiates leave it all behind and are freed to
pursue their Gnosis.

One of the female devotees in the Bacchae sings: Then streams
the earth with milk, yes, streams with wine and nectar of the bee.
And through the air dim perfume steams of Syrian frankincense; and
he, our leader, from his thyrsus spray a torchlight tosses high and
higher, a torchlight like a beacon-fire. To waken all that faint and
stray; and sets them leaping as he sings, his tresses rippling to the sky.

Milk and honey, wine, frankincense, along with an appearing
long haired (his tresses) god that is glowing like a beacon of fire could
apply to Jesus as well as to Dionysus.

Mark 1:6 And John was clothed with camel's hair, and with a
girdle of a skin about his loins; and he did eat locusts and wild honey;

The way John is introduced resembles the way the Maenads
dressed and lived, wearing skins and eating honey and living away
from civilization.

Euripides paints the scene: Come with the voice of timbrel and
drum; let the cry of your joyance uplift and embolden the God of the
joy-cry; with pealing of pipes and with Phrygian clamour. On, where
the vision of holiness thrills, and the music climbs and the maddening
glamour. With the White Maids, to the hills, to the hills!

Homeless – Back to Nature

Dionysus instructs Pentheus: Lonely and untried thy path from
hence shall be, and I thy guide!

Matthew 7:14 Because strait is the gate, and narrow is the way,
which leadeth unto life, and few there be that find it.

Off the beaten path, no longer following the herd, dancing to the beat of a different drummer, the piper calls those who can respond to leave behind the normal life in town and set out on a vision quest journey to find spiritual truths. Initiation takes a great paradigm shifting, a clinging to the new and abandoning of the old. It is beyond logic and reason, but it is heartfelt and experienced transformation. It requires more unlearning than learning, more letting go than acquiring.

Dionysus sings: Damsels uplifted to wander where I wander, and to sleep where I sleep.

Matthew 8:20 And Jesus saith unto him, the foxes have holes, and the birds of the air have nests; but the Son of man hath not where to lay his head.

Devotees to Dionysus sing: To the dear lone lands untroubled of men, where no voice sounds, and amid the shadowy green the little things of the woodland live unseen. What else is wisdom? What of man's endeavor or god's high grace, so lovely and so great? To stand from fear set free, to breathe and wait; to hold a hand uplifted over hate; and shall not loveliness be loved for ever?

Thomas 113 His disciples said to him, "When will the kingdom come?" Jesus said, "It will not come by waiting for it. It will not be a matter of saying, 'here it is' or 'there it is'. Rather, the kingdom of the father is spread out upon the earth, and men do not see it."

Not defined by them, not controlled by them, not seen by them, yet ever present is the other worldly power wielded by Dionysus, by Jesus.

Euripides has in song in his play: Happy he, on the weary sea, who hath fled the tempest and won the haven. Happy whoso hath risen, free, above his striven. For strangely graven is the orb of life, that one and another in gold and power may outpass his brother. And men in their millions float and flow and seethe with a million hopes as leaven; and they win their Will, or they miss their Will, and the hopes are dead or are pined for still; but whoever can know, as the long days go, to live is happy, hath found his heaven!

Mark 4:37-40 And there arose a great storm of wind, and the waves beat into the ship, so that it was now full. And he was in the hinder part of the ship, asleep on a pillow: and they awake him, and say unto him, Master, carest thou not that we perish? And he arose, and rebuked the wind, and said unto the sea, Peace, be still. And the wind ceased, and there was a great calm. And he said unto them, why are ye so fearful? How is it that ye have no faith?

Both Dionysus and Jesus are presented as foreign wandering misfits, alien to the normal culture and interactions of the civilized world. Both offer freedom from the reality in control. Both seek those who can redefine themselves, recast themselves in a different light and purpose. Both calm the storms of so-called civilization which are impeding spiritual happiness, tranquility, peace of mind.

Hold up your Wand

Mark 10:21 Then Jesus beholding him loved him, and said unto him, One thing thou lackest: go thy way, sell whatsoever thou hast, and give to the poor, and thou shalt have treasure in heaven: and come, take up the cross, and follow me.

Take up the cross, I don't think, is encouraging martyrdom, as in a cross of execution. The word is "stake" and reminds me of the mention of the wand, thyrsus, of Dionysus, the planted in the ground symbol of the presence of the direct connection with the new god. Get rid of all ties and connections, find your secluded sacred place, plant your "stake" there and direct connect to the new experience.

Euripides describes each devotee of Dionysus as holding a wand in their right hand, pointing it upwards to the sky in time with the right foot's spring in the sacred dancing. The wand is pictured in ancient drawings and statues as a tall reed with a pine cone on the top. A wand with snakes wrapped around it became the ancient Greek symbol for healing, a variation of which is used today as a sign of the medical profession. To carry the sacred wand meant to be part of the Dionysus movement. Seen through the Dionysus lens, the "take up the cross, and follow me" directive of Jesus means to hold up your wand of membership, your symbolic link to the new movement.

Teiresias is and old blind prophet who seeks after Dionysus with Cadmus. He comments: Thebes is blinded. Thou and I can see. The god himself shall guide! Have thou no care.

Luke 7:22 Then Jesus answering said unto them, Go your way, and tell John what things ye have seen and heard; how that the blind see, the lame walk, the lepers are cleansed, the deaf hear, the dead are raised, to the poor the gospel is preached.

Dionysus was known for the physical strength and healing powers of his devotees. Euripides describes the effect of devotion on the participant: A mysterious strength and exaltation enter into him. The dim years fall from off me! Light am I and young.

Women Devotees

Luke 8:2-3 And certain women, which had been healed of evil spirits and infirmities, Mary called Magdalene, out of whom went seven devils, And Joanna the wife of Chuza Herod's steward, and Susanna, and many others, which ministered unto him of their substance.

In the Bacchae, the female devotees to Dionysus are stereotyped as fanatical, sometimes even dangerous, emotionally connected transformed people. Jesus is also noted for having female devotees, noted as having experienced altered states of being possessed. In the Gnostic tradition, preserved by the Cathars, Mary Magdalene was the wisest of the disciples of Jesus. Perhaps even the whole "seven devils coming out of her" was a reference to a state of advanced initiation: Mary, host to the seven Aeons of the Cosmos that proceed out of her in power, or something like that.

In many ancient and even modern religious traditions, women are given no active role of any meaning. The Dionysus of the Bacchae and the Jesus of the Gospel stand in contrast to the male only religions.

Pentheus, the king of Thebes that opposes Dionysus, sings in lament: Our own wives, our own sisters, from their hearths are flow to wild and secret rites; and cluster there high on the shadowy hills, with dance and prayer to adore this new-made god.

Mystery Music

Dionysus sings: Wake the old sweet sound, the clang that I and mystic Rhea found, the timbrel of the mountain! Gather all Thebes to your song.

Luke 7:32 They are like unto children sitting in the marketplace, and calling one to another, and saying, We have piped unto you, and ye have not danced; we have mourned to you, and ye have not wept.

Music has become associated with Christianity. People gather in churches to play and sing music. Music is a spiritual force. The piper's calling you to join him.

Euripides sets the scene in the Bacchae: Eastern women, the light of the sunrise streaming upon their long white robes and ivy-bound hair. They wear fawn-skins over the robes, and carry some of them timbrels, some pipes and other instruments. Many bear the thyrsus, or sacred wand, made of reed ringed with ivy.

Secret

The Bacchae: They enter stealthily till they see that the place is empty, and then begin their mystic song of worship.

Matthew 6:6 But thou, when thou prayest, enter into thy closet, and when thou hast shut thy door, pray to thy Father which is in secret; and thy Father which seeth in secret shall reward thee openly.

To see that the place is empty and private, the outside world shut out, where the secret is safe, the Mystery protected, is the required setting for the singing to begin.

Thomas 62 Jesus said, "It is to those who are worthy of my mysteries that I tell my mysteries. Do not let your left hand know what your right hand is doing."

Matthew 14:23 And when he had sent the multitudes away, he went up into a mountain apart to pray: and when the evening was come, he was there alone.

White Robes

Dionysus tricks Pentheus into disguising himself as one of the devotees by supplying him with a rich and trailing robe of fine linen.

Dialogue of the Saviour 50 You will rule over the archons. Ridding yourself of jealousy, you will be clothed in light and enter the bridal chamber.

Dialogue of the Saviour 52 The clothing of Life is given to the one who has discovered the Way by which he will leave.

It is interesting that white robes of those devoted to Dionysus equate easily to the "clothed in light" wedding garment hinted at by the Dialogue of the Saviour, a text of early Gnostic Christians.

Shepherd of Hermas Parable 9 15:2 The first is Faith, and the second, Continence, and the third, Power, and the fourth, Longsuffering. But the others stationed between them have these names—Simplicity, Guilelessness, Purity, Cheerfulness, Truth, Understanding, Concord, Love. He that beareth these names and the name of the Son of God shall be able to enter into the kingdom of God.

In the Ninth Parable of the Shepherd of Hermas, Christ and the Twelve Apostles become the Shepherd and the Twelve Virgins. It is the wearing of these virtues that is the wedding garment. At the end of the Shepherd of Hermas we find Hermas waiting the night with the Twelve Virgins for the return of the Shepherd. There are also Twelve Wicked Women which can inappropriately clothe the person and apparently disqualify oneself from the feast. The "bind and throw far away into the darkness" is paralleled in the Shepherd of Hermas as the casting out of the stones that proved not bright enough or whole enough to be useful in building the symbolic tower of the Church.

Shepherd of Hermas Parable 9 15:3 "Hear," saith he, "likewise the names of the women that wear the black garments. Of these also four are more powerful than the rest; the first is Unbelief; the second, Intemperance; the third, Disobedience; the fourth, Deceit; and their followers are called, Sadness, Wickedness, Wantonness, Irascibility, Falsehood, Folly, Slander, Hatred. The servant of God that beareth these names shall see the kingdom of God, but shall not enter into it."

Matthew 22:11-14 And when the king came in to see the guests, he saw there a man which had not on a wedding garment: And he saith unto him, Friend, how camest thou in hither not having a wedding garment? And he was speechless. Then said the king to the servants, Bind him hand and foot, and take him away, and cast him into outer darkness, there shall be weeping and gnashing of teeth. For many are called, but few are chosen.

There are special "habits" worn by monks and nuns, both Catholic and Buddhist. These simple clothes stand in contrast with the material world and the dress of living in cities. Euripides plays with the tradition and in his play the robed devotes to Dionysus notice and attack anyone found in their sacred woods that was not dressed like them. Dionysus suggests that Pentheus dress like one of them to fool them, but his hypocrisy was easily noticed.

Matthew 11:7 And as they departed, Jesus began to say unto the multitudes concerning John, What went ye out into the wilderness to see? A reed shaken with the wind?

A reed, thyrsus, was shaken in the air in time to the dancing of the sacred music.

Matthew 11:8 But what went ye out for to see? A man clothed in soft raiment? Behold, they that wear soft clothing are in kings' houses.

The theme of dressing softly as a requirement and as a pretense, true devotion and hypocrisy, acceptance and rejection is woven through both the Bacchae and the Gospel. In the end both Pentheus and John lose their heads. They both played the part, but failed to be actual devotees to the god. John didn't become a disciple of Jesus, never followed him around. He was a hypocrite, like Pentheus.

Snakes: The Serpent of Eden

Bacchae: Then a horned god was found, and a god with serpents crowned; and for that are serpents wound in the wands his maidens bear, and the songs of serpents sound in the mazes of their hair.

In the modern world we have been conditioned by centuries of "concept manipulation and control" by the churches to equate a horned god and snakes with evil. Snakes wrapped around a wand is the symbol of healing as seen used in the medical profession to this day. One form of early Christianity equated Christ with the wise serpent of Eden who presented humanity with the fruit of Gnosis. And while the "horned one" brings images of the Christian caricature of "Satan gone bad", going back to ancient times the horns represented strength in the wild, purity, and nature.

The snake is a symbol for Christ, the wise serpent of Eden, pushing humanity to partake of knowledge, to take responsibility for our condition, to outgrow the superstitions and fears.

The Testimony of Truth (Nag Hammadi Library IX,3) asks: Why then, do you err and not seek after these mysteries which were prefigured for our sake? Returning to the Eden story, the text goes on to point out that the serpent was wise and God maliciously refused humanity to partake of the tree of knowledge. God cursed the serpent, called him "devil", and set out to cause human minds to become blind that they may neither know nor comprehend the things that are said. Then after God had cursed his people to death, he set up a bronze pole with a serpent (Numbers 21:9) and whoever believes in this serpent will be saved. This serpent is Christ. The point of this early Gnostic Christian writer, Julius Cassianus, is that the ignorance-loving God of the books of Moses had to end up calling on the same serpent that he had once cursed in Eden, the Christ representing a higher power than he could ever control, ever understand. Christ gives the saving Gnosis, the direction, the vision, the freedom from the constraints of ignorance and the ill effects of an oppressive religious culture.

Numbers 21:8 And the LORD said unto Moses, Make thee a fiery serpent, and set it upon a pole: and it shall come to pass, that every one that is bitten, when he looketh upon it, shall live.

When the wandering lost in the desert starving to death "faithful" came to doubt Yaldabaoth, he sent fiery serpent dragons to bite them and caused many to die (Numbers 21:4-6). The serpent on a pole image was the antidote for the plague sent by the Jewish god (Numbers 21:6). That the serpent came to represent Jesus and the image of the serpent with a pole was symbolic of Dionysus is of interest in viewing this ancient Hebrew verse through this lens. Jesus is the antidote serpent on a stick.

John 3:14 And as Moses lifted up the serpent in the wilderness, even so must the Son of man be lifted up:

Matthew 10:16 Behold, I send you forth as sheep in the midst of wolves: be ye therefore wise as serpents, and harmless as doves.

Mark 16:18 They shall take up serpents; and if they drink any deadly thing, it shall not hurt them; they shall lay hands on the sick, and they shall recover.

The dancing with snakes was part of the Mysteries of Dionysus. The power of the healing god was said to be with his devotees, protecting them from becoming sick and enabling them to heal the sick.

Whose Side are you on?

Bacchae: Thebes hath over me no sway! None save him I obey, Dionysus, child of the highest, him I obey and adore!

Luke 21:15 For I will give you a mouth and wisdom, which all your adversaries shall not be able to gainsay nor resist.

The idea that once you embrace the new god, this places you at odds with your old city. You choose Dionysus over Thebes, Jesus over Jerusalem. It puts you on the spot to have to defend your choice, define and admit whose side you are on. There is also this sense of being superior, of having a powerful connection to a source of wisdom that the non-devotees are missing out on.

Appeal to the City

Dionysus returns to Thebes as a stranger, a foreigner, even though he should have been their beloved chosen son, miraculously born from one of their own and yet, at the same time, the child of

Zeus Almighty. Dionysus sings: I cry this Thebes to waken. Set her hands to clasp my wand, mine ivied javelin, and round her shoulders hang my wild fawn-skin.

There is a Nag Hammadi Library text called Allogenes (XI,3), the word means foreigner or stranger. The stranger is encountered within us, the triple strength force that is stronger than God. This force is from a place beyond substance, higher than perfection, that realm Plato imagined to exist beyond the material world. This encounter empowers those who can express it with the Gnosis of vitality, mentality, and the understanding of the "That which is" which is beyond the normal way of thinking. It is alien, but more real than reality.

Matthew 23:37: O Jerusalem, Jerusalem, thou that killest the prophets, and stonest them which are sent unto thee, how often would I have gathered thy children together, even as a hen gathereth her chickens under her wings, and ye would not!

In both the Bacchae and the Gospel there is a sense of wishing to connect, to gather and hold and decorate and protect. The symbolism of feeding and supplying are at play in many ancient myths. Planting and harvesting are important. The force of nature to grow and thrive, to take seeds and produce grain for bread, grapes for wine, was considered magical and sacred and supplied by divine forces of gods and goddesses looking over humanity and protecting us from famine and hunger.

Luke 13:28-30 There shall be weeping and gnashing of teeth, when ye shall see Abraham, and Isaac, and Jacob, and all the prophets, in the kingdom of God, and you yourselves thrust out. And they shall come from the east, and from the west, and from the north, and from the south, and shall sit down in the kingdom of God. And, behold, there are last which shall be first, and there are first which shall be last.

The idea that Jesus should belong to Jerusalem, the holy city, but instead he is known and respected in so many places except for Jerusalem is like how Thebes should have embraced their internationally famous son, Dionysus.

In the trial of Dionysus, Pentheus asks: Comest thou first to Thebes, to have thy god established? Dionysus explains: Nay; all Barbary hath trod his dance ere this. Pentheus replies: A low blind folk, I ween, beside our Hellenes! Dionysus enlightens: Higher and more keen in this thing, though their ways are not thy way. In this way the last become first, the gentiles receive the Jewish Messiah. The holy city, that should embrace her special son, misses the opportunity.

Thomas 68: Jesus said, "Blessed are you when you are hated and persecuted. Wherever you have been persecuted they will find no place."

The Jerusalem Temple was no more, knocked down, the once "built up ground' leveled, the ancient Jewish sacred center replaced by Hadrian with temples dedicated to Jupiter and Venus. You could still stand on the Mount of Olives, but no longer find anything resembling the ancient temple.

Josephus: The Antiquities of the Jews, Book 20, Chapter 8, Paragraph 6 in part: Moreover, there came out of Egypt about this time to Jerusalem, one that said he was a prophet, and advised the multitude of the common people to go along with him to the Mount of Olives, as it was called, which lay over against the city, and at the distance of five furlongs. He said farther, that he would show them from hence, how, at his command, the walls of Jerusalem would fall down; and he promised that he would procure them an entrance into the city through those walls, when they were fallen down.

Living Fountain

The women devotees to Dionysus sing in the Bacchae: Oh, blessed he in all wise, who hath drunk the Living Fountain, whose life no folly staineth, and his soul is near to God; whose sins are lifted, pall-wise, and he worships on the Mountain and where Cybele ordaineth, our Mother, he has trod: his head with ivy laden and his thyrsus tossing high.

AL SAFFAT 37.45-46 Round will be passed to them a Cup from a clear-flowing fountain, Crystal-white, of a taste delicious to those who drink (thereof),

AL INSAN 76.6 A Fountain where the Devotees of Allah do drink, making it flow in unstinted abundance.

Clear, delicious, abundant Holy Water for all. Clean water is a luxury when living in ancient times in the desert areas. To find fresh water was to find the source for being alive. This explains why the spiritual symbolism of water transcends cultures and ages.

Odes of Solomon 6:10-18 For it spread over the face of all the earth, and it filled everything. Then all the thirsty upon the earth drank, and thirst was relieved and quenched; for from the Most High the drink was given. Blessed, therefore, are the ministers of that drink, who have been entrusted with his water. They have pleased the parched lips, and have restored the paralyzed will, even lives who were about to expire, they have seized from Death, and members who had fallen, they have restored and set up. They gave power for their coming, and light for their eyes. Because everyone recognized them as the Lord's, and lived by the living water of eternity.

John 7:38 He that believeth on me, as the scripture hath said, out of his belly shall flow rivers of living water.

Isaiah 12:3 Therefore with joy shall ye draw water out of the wells of salvation.

Salvation in Hebrew is the word that can be translated as Joshua, which is in the Greek LXX translation the name that is translated into English as Jesus. Early Christian writers considered that every occurrence of this word in Jewish scriptures was a reference to Jesus. This is a good find for them, for it equates Jesus with the concept of dying of thirst and discovering a hidden spring of fresh life-giving water. Dionysus offers the sacred wine to uplift the spirits of humanity. Jesus, to go one better, offers the sacred water in the desert that is required for life itself.

Revelation 7:17 For the Lamb which is in the midst of the throne shall feed them, and shall lead them unto living fountains of waters: and God shall wipe away all tears from their eyes.

Thomas 108 Jesus said, "He who will drink from my mouth will become like me. I myself shall become he, and the things that are hidden will be revealed to him."

John 4:10 Jesus answered and said unto her, If thou knewest the gift of God, and who it is that saith to thee, Give me to drink; thou wouldest have asked of him, and he would have given thee living water.

John 4:14 But whosoever drinketh of the water that I shall give him shall never thirst; but the water that I shall give him shall be in him a well of water springing up into everlasting life.

Euripides imagines: One would raise her wand and smite the rock, and straight a jet of quick bright water came. Another set her thyrsus in the bosomed earth, and there was red wine that the god sent up to her.

John 19:34 But one of the soldiers with a spear pierced his side, and forthwith came there out blood and water.

1 John 5:6-8 This is he that came by water and blood, even Jesus Christ; not by water only, but by water and blood. And it is the Spirit that beareth witness, because the Spirit is truth. For there are three that bear record in heaven, the Father, the Word, and the Holy Ghost: and these three are one. And there are three that bear witness in earth, the Spirit, and the water, and the blood: and these three agree in one.

Early Christianity was rife with such symbolism.

Sacred Wine

In the Dionysus tradition, the fountain of the god was one of supplying the sacred wine for the devotees. The bread represented the body of the goddess of the grain, but the wine was the blood of Dionysus, the merciful gift of the young god to humanity.

John 2:2-3 And both Jesus was called, and his disciples, to the marriage. And when they wanted wine, the mother of Jesus saith unto him, they have no wine.

John 2:9-10 When the ruler of the feast had tasted the water that was made wine, and knew not whence it was: (but the servants which drew the water knew;) the governor of the feast called the bridegroom, And saith unto him, Every man at the beginning doth set forth good wine; and when men have well drunk, then that which is worse: but thou hast kept the good wine until now.

Jesus magically supplying the wine for the "marriage feast" links him in role to Dionysus, the god of wine. Euripides notes that high on the shadowy hills deep wine-jars stand. The drinking of this blood of Dionysus, the wine, took on a sacramental meaning for the devotees, and the very concept offers symbolic meaning for those who embrace the story. Thus we understand the focus of the Eucharist in Catholic mass.

Bread and Wine

In the Bacchae, Teiresias, the old prophet, explains: Two spirits there be that in man's world are first of worth. Demeter one is named, she is the earth who feeds man's frame with sustenance of things dry. Second, is the power from Semele born. He found the liquid shower hid in the grape. He rests man's spirit dim from grieving, when the vine exalteth him. He giveth sleep to sink the fretful day in cool forgetting. Is there any way with man's sore heart, save only to forget. Yes, being God, the blood of him is set before the gods in sacrifice, that we for his sake may be blest.

In the feasts of men comes his crowned slumber; then pain is dead and hate forgiven!

Bread from the goddess and wine from the god.

1 Corinthians 11:23-29 For I have received of the Lord that which also I delivered unto you, That the Lord Jesus the same night in which he was betrayed took bread: And when he had given thanks, he brake it, and said, Take, eat: this is my body, which is broken for you: this do in remembrance of me. After the same manner also he took the cup, when he had supped, saying, this cup is the new testament in my blood: this do ye, as oft as ye drink it, in remembrance of me. For as often as ye eat this bread, and drink this cup, ye do shew the Lord's death till he come. Wherefore whosoever shall eat this bread, and drink this cup of the Lord, unworthily, shall be guilty of the body and blood of the Lord. But let a man examine himself, and so let him eat of that bread, and drink of that cup. For he that eateth and drinketh unworthily, eateth and drinketh damnation to himself, not discerning the Lord's body.

John 6:53-57 Then Jesus said unto them, Verily, verily, I say unto you, Except ye eat the flesh of the Son of man, and drink his blood, ye have no life in you. Whoso eateth my flesh, and drinketh my blood, hath eternal life; and I will raise him up at the last day. For my flesh is meat indeed, and my blood is drink indeed. He that eateth my flesh, and drinketh my blood, dwelleth in me, and I in him. As the living Father hath sent me, and I live by the Father: so he that eateth me, even he shall live by me.

Christianity obviously doesn't have the goddess part of the equation. In Gnosticism, the Holy Spirit is understood as the Mother, but in Catholic based Christianity, the Holy Spirit is genderless. Thus the eating as well as the drinking is linked to the god. The way Christianity turned out, there is no goddess, and thus both the bread and the wine are linked to Jesus alone.

God the Sower

The women devotees to Dionysus sing in the Bacchae: Oh, bring the Joy-bestower, God-seed of God the Sower.

In the Bacchae there is the context of the god beyond the god at hand, the Zeus parent of Dionysus.

Matthew 13:24-25 Another parable put he forth unto them, saying, The kingdom of heaven is likened unto a man which sowed good seed in his field: But while men slept, his enemy came and sowed tares among the wheat, and went his way.

There is a tradition in Orphic myth, reflected in the writings of Nonnus and Callimachus, where the Titans are sent by Hera to consume Dionysus. Zeus becomes angry and destroys the Titans. From the ashes of the destroyed Titans, who had consumed Dionysus, we are created. Dionysus was subsequently reborn, but parts of him remain in the material from which our bodies are made. Dionysus is like having a sacred seed planted in our physical mortal natures, an inner stream of power that allows us to transcend, an inner light to show us the way. We are caught between the ignorant forces of the Titans and the seed of God planted in each of us. How we harvest ourselves determines if Dionysus (the seed of God) wins out or rather the Titans (the dark weed tares elemental forces of physical nature).

Back from the Dead

Cadmus speaks in the Bacchae: His is the soul of that dead life of old that spring from mine own daughter? Surely must thou and I with all the strength of men exalt him.

Cadmus was the father of Semele, the human mother of Dionysus. He is surprised that the dead child was now returned alive. Dionysus was thought to have died along with his mother, but protected by Zeus and born again. In the Gospel the death of Jesus is placed as the result of his trial and execution. No mortal trial could even imprison Dionysus, much less execute him.

The being "born again" of Dionysus is mentioned in the Bacchae: Zeus, the Lord of Wonder, devised new hairs of birth, yes, his own flesh tore to hide him, and with clasps of bitter gold did a secret son enfold. And the Queen knew not beside him; till the perfect hour was there; then a horned God was found, and a god with serpents crowned.

The Queen, the goddess Hera, was ignorant.

John 1:2-5 The same was in the beginning with God. All things were made by him; and without him was not any thing made that was made. In him was life; and the life was the light of men. And the light shineth in darkness; and the darkness comprehended it not.

The darkness was ignorant of that which came out of God, through which everything was defined, the force of life and light trapped in the darkness of the material state. Hera, the sender of the Titans to destroy young Dionysus, was ignorant of his second birth to come from the side of Zeus Almighty.

In these ancient thoughts we already find the seed of the Gnostic myth that the force (demiurge, Hera) that rules the material creation (physical being, Titans) is overcome by the god child (Jesus, Dionysus) who shows the way back to the father God (Zeus) in the realm beyond the physical (Pleroma).

Official Plot

Disbelieved Claim

Pentheus in the Bacchae reasons: Tis all his word, this tale of Dionysus; how that same babe that was blasted by the lightning flame with his dead mother, for that mother's lie, was reconceived born perfect from the thigh of Zeus, and now is God! What call ye these? Dreams? Gibes of the unknown wander? Blasphemies.

Matthew 26:63-66 But Jesus held his peace. And the high priest answered and said unto him, I adjure thee by the living God, that thou tell us whether thou be the Christ, the Son of God. Jesus saith unto him, Thou hast said: nevertheless I say unto you, hereafter shall ye see the Son of man sitting on the right hand of power, and coming in the clouds of heaven. Then the high priest rent his clothes, saying, He hath spoken blasphemy; what further need have we of witnesses? Behold, now ye have heard his blasphemy. What think ye? They answered and said, He is guilty of death.

At the end of the Bacchae there is a missing page in the only surviving copy from the ancient world. It is thought to contain a scene after the trial of Dionysus that has the god appearing on a cloud and pronouncing judgment on Thebes. The arriving or departing on a cloud is proof of the divinity of the one who they thought was a mortal man. The equating of the Christ (Messiah) with being the child of God would not be a Jewish thought. The Christ (Messiah) was to be a human king war hero that came to defeat the enemies of the Jews. The way the trial of Jesus for being "Christ, the Son of God" reads would make better sense from the light of the story of Dionysus in Thebes. Jesus was presented as claiming to be the son of a higher god in the same way that Dionysus claimed to be the son of Zeus. This is not being just the child of God, but the child of a God above God. Alien divinity.

Plot to Destroy

Pentheus in the Bacchae plots against Dionysus like the plotting against the devotees to Baal in the Bible: I will go hunt them! Aye, and snare my birds with nets of iron, to quell their prayer and mountain song and rites of rascaldom! Let me grip him once, but once, within these walls, right swift that wand shall cease its music, and that drift of tossing curls lie still when my rude sword falls between neck and trunk!

John 11:49-50 And one of them, named Caiaphas, being the high priest that same year, said unto them, Ye know nothing at all, Nor consider that it is expedient for us, that one man should die for the people, and that the whole nation perish not.

It is interesting that Jesus must die to protect the national security according to Caiaphas. Pentheus explains: All my land is made their mock. This needs an iron hand! The details are fleshed out better as to why Pentheus feared that Dionysus was shaking his entire reality. The original Jesus story, before becoming so soft soaped, must have come across as revolutionary to the entire structure of thought Caiaphas stood upon, the extant of the paradigm at play in which his entire concept of "nation" stood. Jesus was the poison that threatened to turn his world upside down and the only antidote he could imagine was the violent ending of this intruding voice of change.

Matthew 26:3-4 Then assembled together the chief priests, and the scribes, and the elders of the people, unto the palace of the high priest, who was called Caiaphas, And consulted that they might take Jesus by subtilty, and kill him.

Bacchae: Pentheus: Seek amain this girl-faced stranger, that hath wrought such bane to all Thebes, preying on our maids and wives.

Seek till ye find; and lead him in gyves till he be judged and stoned, and weep in blood the day he troubled Pentheus with his God!

John 10:30-33 I and my Father are one. Then the Jews took up stones again to stone him. Jesus answered them, Many good works have I shewed you from my Father; for which of those works do ye stone me? The Jews answered him, saying, for a good work we stone thee not; but for blasphemy; and because that thou, being a man, makest thyself God.

Authorities want to destroy anything that would replace them. Pentheus the king is acting out of fear that Dionysus is more important and powerful than him. Caiaphas the chief priest is acting out of fear that Jesus is more important and powerful than him.

To say that Jesus is one with his Father, which he identifies as the highest god, would make any sense of ordained priesthood lesser in comparison. "You may have memorized the verses, but God is my dad" is a very powerful response. You may be king of Thebes, but my dad is Zeus. It is the same trial situation that Jesus finds himself in as did Dionysus in the Bacchae.

Arrest

Bacchae: Our quest is finished, and thy prey, O king, caught; for the chase was swift, and this wild thing most tame; yet never flinched, nor thought to flee, but held both hands out unresistingly. No change, no blanching of the wine-red cheek. He waited while we came, and bade us wreak all thy decree; yea, laughed.

John 18:4-8 Jesus therefore, knowing all things that should come upon him, went forth, and said unto them, whom seek ye? They answered him, Jesus the Nazarite. Jesus saith unto them, I am he. And Judas also, which betrayed him, stood with them. As soon then as he had said unto them, I am he, they went backward, and fell to the ground. Then asked he them again, whom seek ye? And they said, Jesus the Nazarite. Jesus answered, I have told you that I am he: if therefore ye seek me, let these go their way:

In the Bacchae, the soldiers return explaining that they didn't want to arrest Dionysus, but had to carry out their duty. The stumbling guards of Caiaphas met with an overly cooperative Jesus, Dionysus-like and not at all like a strong war hero Messiah figure. That's the point.

Mock Trial | Image Jesting

Matthew 27:28-29 And they stripped him, and put on him a scarlet robe. And when they had platted a crown of thorns, they put it upon his head, and a reed in his right hand: and they bowed the knee before him, and mocked him, saying, Hail, King of the Jews!

In the trial of Dionysus, he is made to look less like his god self and more like a common person to mockingly prove that he is not really the son of God. In the trial of Jesus, he is made to take on the accessories of Dionysus in jest, a crown of thorns to pretend to be a crown of serpents, and a reed to hold like the wand (thyrsus) of Dionysus.

Bacchae: Pentheus speaks jeeringly. Dionysus remains gentle and unafraid. Pentheus jests: Long curls, withal! That show thou never hast been a wrestler!

Mark 14:60-61 And the high priest stood up in the midst, and asked Jesus, saying, Answerest thou nothing? What is it which these witness against thee? But he held his peace, and answered nothing. Again the high priest asked him, and said unto him, Art thou the Christ, the Son of the Blessed?

The Christ or the Son of the Blessed? Jesus Christ or Jesus Barabbas? The Arriving Messiah of hope for victory through violent revolution or the Alternative God appearing? The Christ or the Anti-Christ who presents himself as being God? The question of Caiaphas echoes throughout the aeon.

Warriors keep short hair so that their opponents may not be able to grab their hair when fighting. Pentheus mocks Dionysus for having long hair and thus not being able to put up much of a fight. In all images of Jesus throughout the centuries, he is presented as having long hair. It is probably in light of this same symbolism of being peaceful and non-threatening.

Bacchae: Pentheus: Thy doom is fixed, for false pretence corrupting Thebes. Dionysus: Not mine; but thine for dense blindness of heart, and for blaspheming God!

Pentheus orders the hair of Dionysus cut off and his staff taken away.

Having his hair cut off would explain why the most beloved disciple of Jesus did not recognize him when seeing him resurrected after the trial and execution (John 20:14).

John 20:15-16 Jesus saith unto her, Woman, why weepest thou? Whom seekest thou? She, supposing him to be the gardener, saith unto him, Sir, if thou have borne him hence, tell me where thou hast laid him, and I will take him away. Jesus saith unto her, Mary. She turned herself, and saith unto him, Rabboni; which is to say, Master.

Dionysus vows: My Lord God will unloose me, when I speak the word.

Matthew 26:53 Thinkest thou that I cannot now pray to my Father, and he shall presently give me more than twelve legions of angels?

The god mocks the mortal trial's supposed power over the captive.

Escape

Dionysus frees himself and calls for his faithful: Awake, ye damsels; hear my cry. Calling my chosen; hearken ye!

He explains how he tricked Pentheus into seeing Dionysus after he had escaped: he smote at emptiness, stabbed in the air, and strove in wrath, as though it were me he slew.

Luke 4:28-30 And all they in the synagogue, when they heard these things, were filled with wrath, And rose up, and thrust him out of the city, and led him unto the brow of the hill whereon their city was built, that they might cast him down headlong. But he passing through the midst of them went his way,

The walking right through a large hostile crowd could be interpreted as a Docetist view of Jesus as only appearing to be really human. This is a hint at how Jesus escapes death. The walking through walls, walking on water, appearing out of nowhere and disappearing imply that Jesus was not a normal tangible human. The casting down was a story associated with James the brother of Jesus (2 Apocalypse of James in the Nag Hammadi Library).

Earthquake

Bacchae: Dionysus speaks: Spirit of the chained earthquake, hear my word; awake, awake! An earthquake suddenly shakes the pillars of the castle of Pentheus. The leader of the followers proclaims: God's child hath come, and all is overthrown!

Matthew 27:51 And, behold, the veil of the temple was rent in twain from the top to the bottom; and the earth did quake, and the rocks rent;

Matthew 27:54 Now when the centurion, and they that were with him, watching Jesus, saw the earthquake, and those things that were done, they feared greatly, saying, Truly this was the Son of God.

Matthew 28:2 And, behold, there was a great earthquake: for the angel of the Lord descended from heaven, and came and rolled back the stone from the door, and sat upon it.

The Jesus story goes beyond the Dionysus story in that he doesn't just escape being held in prison, he escapes the state of being dead.

Released

The name "bar" "abbas" means Son of the Father. Some manuscripts of Matthew 27:16 read "Jesus Barabbas". The name "Jesus" was removed and today there are only 6 Greek, 2 Syrian, and 1 Armenian versions that preserve "Jesus" in this verse. Now why was the distinction and choice given here between killing or freeing "Jesus Son of the Father" and "Jesus Christ of the Jews"? Could the "Christ of the Jews" be a reference to one or all of the Messianic pretenders like Simon bar Kokhba? Which Messianic tradition do you people want? Was he the authentic heir to the tradition of xenophobia and terrorist style revolutionary movements? Or was he the "Son of the Father" teacher of pacifist openness to intercultural harmony and a spiritual mindset that can transcend Judaism? There is something confusing going on in the very question something observed by dogmatic assertions of church fathers editing earlier texts to ensure they contained no noticeable heresy.

Matthew 27:16-17 And they had then a notable prisoner, called Jesus Barabbas. Therefore when they were gathered together, Pilate said unto them, Whom will ye that I release unto you? Barabbas, or Jesus which is called Christ?

Josephus: The Antiquities of the Jews, Book 18, Chapter 3, Paragraph 1 in part: Pilate…in order to abolish the Jewish laws…introduced Caesar's effigies, which were upon the ensigns, and brought them into the city; whereas our law forbids us the very making of images.

Whose side was Pilate on? Pilate supported Caesar against the Jews that objected and would revolt. Which "Jesus" savior leader concept would he help and which would he kill? Jesus son of the Father was released while Jesus Messiah was executed.

Second Treatise of the Great Seth (Nag Hammadi VII,2), Jesus explains: I did not die in reality but in appearance. For my death, which they think happened, happened to them in their error and blindness, since they nailed their man unto their death. It was another, their father, who drank the gall and the vinegar; it was not I. They struck me with the reeds; it was another, Simon, who bore the cross on his shoulders. It was another upon whom they placed the crown of thorns. But I was rejoicing in the height. I was laughing at their ignorance.   Apocalypse of Peter (Nag Hammadi VII,3) has Jesus explaining to Peter: He whom they crucified is the first-born, and the home of demons, and the stony vessel in which they dwell, of Elohim, of the cross which is under the Law. But he who stands near him is the living Savior, the first in him, whom they seized and released, who stands joyfully looking at those who did him violence, while they are divided among themselves. Therefore he laughs at their lack of perception. He whom you saw on the tree, glad and laughing, this is the living Jesus.

The whole "they crucified the wrong person" theme in Gnostic stories leaves us with an interesting observation. If the real Jesus didn't die, then there is no symbolic salvation from the bleeding death of the wrong Jesus, unless it is in that the Messianic hopes for revolution against the Romans is now dead. It was Simon who actually died, Simon bar Kokhba, the flesh and blood Messiah warrior. Jesus is of a kingdom not of this world. He cannot die. He is the dream and hope for a future better world guided by love and peace.

Interesting that the Qur'an rejects that Jesus was even crucified, much less resurrected. He was indeed rejected, but miraculously protected by God. In this, Muhammad agrees with the Gnostic traditions.

AL MA'IDAH 5.110: And behold! I did restrain the Children of Israel from violence to thee [Jesus] when thou didst show them the clear signs, and the unbelievers among them said: "This is nothing but evident magic."

AL NISA 4.157: That they said (in boast) "We killed Christ Jesus the son of Mary, the Messenger of Allah" – but they killed him not, nor crucified him, but so it was made to appear to them, and those who differ therein are full of doubts, with no certain knowledge, but only conjecture to follow, for of a surety they killed him not – nay,

Allah raised him up unto Himself; and Allah is exalted in Power, Wise.

Revenge Mode

Euripides sums up the Bacchae: Pray for this poor city, that the righteous God move not in anger.

O there is grace, and there is the heart's desire, and peace to adore thee, thou spirit of guiding fire! A god of heaven is he, and born in majesty; yet hath he mirth in the joy of the earth, and he loveth constantly her who brings increase. The feeder of children, peace. No grudge hath he of the great; no scorn of the mean estate; but to all that liveth his wine he giveth, griefless, immaculate; only on them that spurn joy, may his anger burn.

Luke 19:41-44 And when he was come near, he beheld the city, and wept over it, Saying, If thou hadst known, even thou, at least in this thy day, the things which belong unto thy peace! But now they are hid from thine eyes. For the days shall come upon thee, that thine enemies shall cast a trench about thee, and compass thee round, and keep thee in on every side, And shall lay thee even with the ground, and thy children within thee; and they shall not leave in thee one stone upon another; because thou knewest not the time of thy visitation.

Bacchae: Teiresias the prophet explains: Prophecy cleaves to all frenzy, but beyond all else to frenzy of prayer. Then in us verily dwells the god himself, and speaks the thing to be. Yea, and of Are's realm a part hath he. When mortal armies, mailed and arrayed, have in strange fear, or ever blade met blade, fled maddened, tis this god that palsied them.

The same god that inspires joy and peace and love can inspire fear and hatred and anger and violence. Christian history is lined with crusades, inquisitions and witch hunts. This is the ultimate tragedy of interacting with the presence of a god. The embracing bliss may be very sweet, but the reacting revenge on the state of being rejected is an intensity just as strong.

Matthew 10:34-36 Think not that I am come to send peace on earth: I came not to send peace, but a sword. For I am come to set a man at variance against his father, and the daughter against her mother, and the daughter in law against her mother in law. And a man's foes shall be they of his own household.

Bacchae: Pentheus shouts: Away, and tie him where the steads are tied; aye, let him lie in the manger! Dionysus taunts Pentheus after the guards tied him up: I having vision and ye blind! He whom thou deniest cometh after thee for recompense.

In the Gospel, Jesus talks about himself in the third person, just as Dionysus does here. His prophecies of the "son of man" coming sound like he is talking about someone other than himself. In both the Bacchae and the Gospel, the audience understands that the condemned man on trial and the avenging godlike man to return for justice are one and the same.

Luke 18:8 I tell you that he will avenge them speedily. Nevertheless when the Son of man cometh, shall he find faith on the earth?

Matthew 16:28 Verily I say unto you, There be some standing here, which shall not taste of death, till they see the Son of man coming in his kingdom.

In the Jesus story, it was Titus who came within the lifetime of some present, 40 years later in the year 70. But the Jesus story works in two dimensions at once, the physical reality of the fate of physical Jerusalem, and the spiritual reality of the kingdom not of this world with its "New Jerusalem".

Revelation 3:12 Him that overcometh will I make a pillar in the temple of my God, and he shall go no more out: and I will write upon him the name of my God, and the name of the city of my God, *which is* **new Jerusalem**, which cometh down out of heaven from my God: and *I will write upon him* my **new** name.

Matthew 24:30 And then shall appear the sign of the Son of man in heaven: and then shall all the tribes of the earth mourn, and they shall see the Son of man coming in the clouds of heaven with power and great glory.

Matthew 24:43-44 But know this, that if the goodman of the house had known in what watch the thief would come, he would have watched, and would not have suffered his house to be broken up. Therefore be ye also ready: for in such an hour as ye think not the Son of man cometh.

Bacchae: The fate of Pentheus: Then mid his dreams God smote him yet again! He overthrew all that high house. And there in wreck for evermore it lies. That the day of this my bondage may be sore in Pentheus' eyes! And now his sword is fallen, and he lies outworn and wan who dared to rise against his god in wrath, being but man.

When Dionysus descends from the sky on a cloud to the Thebes that had rejected him, he laments: Ah, had ye seen truth in the hour ye would not, all had been well with ye, and the child of God your friend! Agave, the mother of the now dead king Pentheus, responds: Dionysus, we beseech thee! We have sinned! Dionysus answers: Too late! When there was time, ye knew me not. Ye mocked me, being God; this is your wage.

Luke 13:25-27 When once the householder has risen up and shut the door, you will begin to stand outside and to knock at the door, saying, 'Lord, open to us.' He will answer you, 'I do not know where you come from.' Then shall ye begin to say, We have eaten and drunk in thy presence, and thou hast taught in our streets. But he shall say, I tell you, I know you not whence ye are; depart from me, all ye workers of iniquity.

Ascension

Dionysus rises upon the cloud and disappears.

Luke 24:51 And it came to pass, while he blessed them, he was parted from them, and carried up into heaven.

In the end Thebes sees its rulers destroyed, its people sent out into exile.

Bacchae: On all this house, in bitter wise, our lord and master, Dionyse, hath poured the utter dregs of pain!

In the year 135, Hadrian exiled all Jews from Jerusalem, renamed the city Aelia Capitolina, set up a statue of himself at the site of the Temple that had been destroyed, erected a Temple devoted to Jupiter (Father Zeus) at the same site, and erected a Temple devoted to Venus (Aphrodite; Love). Jews were forbidden to visit the reformed city.

Formula

A god that is the protagonist of the story.

A god that is both child of the ultimate God and of mortal human mother.

A god that appears to be normal human that only those who have been enlightened to the truth understand his true identity.

A god fought against and put on trial by the authorities representing civilized human culture.

A god who directly connects to and transforms those who desire the experience.

Titus

Josephus: The Wars of the Jews, Book 5, Chapter 5: explains that the destruction of Jerusalem was a direct result of false prophets who said they spoke for God, rallying the people to gather at the temple and have faith that they should "receive miraculous signs of their deliverance" and be successful in standing up against the Roman Empire. "Without either eyes to see, or minds to consider" the actual signs from the actual God. "For, before sunsetting, chariots and troops of soldiers in their armor were seen running about among the clouds, and surrounding of cities." Josephus continues that on the day of Pentecost "the priests felt a quaking, and heard a great noise, and after that they heard a sound as of a great multitude, saying, 'Let us remove hence.'" A wise man named Jesus shouted, "A voice from the east, a voice from the west, a voice from the four winds, a voice against Jerusalem and the holy house, a voice against the bridegrooms and the brides, and a voice against this whole people!" Josephus considered, "God takes care of mankind, and by all ways possible foreshows to our race what is for their preservation; but that men perish by those miseries which they madly and voluntarily bring upon themselves.

Josephus: The Wars of the Jews, Book 5, Chapter 6: continues his account of Titus conquering Jerusalem: "So Titus charged his soldiers to restrain their rage, and to let their darts alone, and appointed an interpreter between them, which was a sign that he was the conqueror." The victorious Titus gives speech to the defeated Jewish rebellion, explaining that he found the people to love peace but the few with malicious intent escalated matters into a full on war. He would give sanctuary to any Jews who wanted to abandon the conflict. He continuously proposed peace. He offered them their lives if they would just admit defeat.

It is an amusing turn of events that places Titus as the savior of Jerusalem, ridding it of all violence and establishing a city renewed in peace and cosmopolitan appreciation of education and progress. The violence that this arriving "star" had to oppose was not that of foreigners, but that of the most zealous of the faithful chosen people themselves. A lot of the attributes of Titus, being hesitant to use violence as the solution, seeking terms of peace, looking for divine signs of a much larger and more inclusive scope, are applied to the Jesus of the Gospel story.

Orphic Theogonies

Hesiod and other ancient writers told the same story. Dionysus, the son of Zeus (same as Jupiter for the Romans), was victim to the rage of the goddess Hera. Hera instructs the Titans to kill and eat baby Dionysus. Athena (same as Minerva for the Romans; Wisdom) manages to save the sacred heart of Dionysus, but the Titans had consumed the rest. Zeus destroys the Titans and the resulting ashes contained remnants of the consumed Dionysus. Out of these ashes we have been created. The soul of man (Dionysus factor) is therefore divine, but the body (Titan factor) holds the soul in bondage.

The themes of the god's death and resurrection, his consumption by the Titans (Eucharist), and Athena (Wisdom) saving his heart (Sacred Heart of Jesus) play out in the Jesus stories.

Neo-Platonism

Plotinus wrote a text called the Enneads. He explains that our souls come from the Eternal Supreme and we are alienated here and must find a way to return. The One is perfectly good, but beyond the limits of the cosmos we live in. The One can supply "thought energy patterns", but cannot personally descend into our realm. The shadowed descended thoughts approximate the Goodness of The One, becoming the Demiurge Mind. This god in our realm is not the ultimate God. We are caught in between The One and the Demiurge Mind, between a "unity and harmony and love" on the one hand and "conflict and suffering and violence" on the other hand. "Creation is all good" is an obviously wrong statement. "Creation is all evil" is likewise obviously wrong. What we have to do is to reconnect to The One, come to the required Gnosis, become God by participation, as St. John of the Cross expresses (The Spiritual Canticle 31:1). For the Neo-Platonists, this is the process of henosis, the state of perfect movement and rest, being swallowed up in divinity, an ecstatic reunion with the Highest God, the God above God.

There are relationships of thoughts that have been forgotten on purpose. The Christians killed the Neo-Platonism saint, Hypatia of Alexandria. They should have learned from her. She knew the Logos better than they did. The Christians destroyed the Gnostic texts. They should have learned from them. They understood Christ better than what few texts became their Bible. The Sethian Gnostics created a fusion of Neo-Platonism concepts and an inverted study of Jewish scriptures. Neo-Platonism was a philosophical school of thought taking ideas of Plato (died 247 BC) to logical conclusions as to the true nature of God, of ourselves, and how everything relates. Plato, in turn, was influenced by Pythagoras (died 490 BC), whose influence was still felt at the time of the origins of Christianity by the teachings and legends surrounding Apollonius of Tyana (according to Philostratus). Pythagoras was influenced by Orphism, the ancient legends of the Mysteries focused upon Dionysus.

Plotinus, the great Neo-Platonist master, spoke of The One, the ineffable transcendent god, the Divine Mind, from which everything appeared as subsequent realities of emanations. Did the Neo-Platonists influence the Christian Gnostics or was it the other way around (or both)? This thought is radically different from the modern concept of God as being separate from us, above and beyond us. Neo-Platonism is monistic, or rather, panentheistic, meaning that an eternal animating force interpenetrates every part of nature and yet still transcends it all. We are all a part of The One, but The One is more than the sum total of us all. In the Enneads (Plotinus), The One is expressed as being evident in deeds of kindness, of compassion, of love. The One is the perfect goodness above and beyond the Demiurge, the God above God, the Singularity that reabsorbs all diversity. By contrast, the Demiurge generates direction, conquest, conflict, and suffering. The Almighty Demiurge has to be transcended before being absorbed back into the Purity. We, humanity, need to transcend and abandon the latent urge to control and motivate obedience and justify exploitation. The Jewish god would be understood as being the Demiurge from this lens.

Solomon: Baal and Yaldabaoth (Antithesis Twist)

If Dionysus was sought for in Jewish scriptures, he would be found in Baal.

The divine alter ego in modern Christianity is the caricature of "Satan" himself, the guy to blame for the Fundamentalists not taking over the world. Every alternative out there was labeled as this "Satan" figure, from the beloved Roman god of light, Lucifer, back to the ancient lord of the Near East, Baal.

Like two competing political parties, two competing sports teams, two television networks, and everyone takes sides. Yahweh (Yaldabaoth through the Gnostic lens) represented the main franchise conservative ancient tradition, dating back to the legendary conquering heroes of the Promised Land. Baal represented the opposition, the radical "different values" alternative, awakened during the reign of the fabled king Solomon. The whole "it would be better if" dreamer collection of ancient Judaism seemed to bounce back and forth between the two. The Messiah was to be a war hero, defending the chosen people against everyone who is different – the true son of Yaldabaoth. But then again, the Messianic Age to come was to be a revival of the festivities related to Baal, as we shall explore through this lens. The savior figure, whose son was he? What traditions did he represent?

Hosea 2:11-13 is a shot taken by the Yaldabaoth faction against the popularity of the Baal movement. This gives us a snapshot insight of how the Baal people lived and thought, albeit referenced through the words of their enemies. They celebrated with mirth, joy, happiness, and festivals, recognizing new moons and sacred days and holidays. They cherished their grape vines and fig trees, both of which are referenced in the Gospel stories. They burned incense, wore special costumes with earrings and jewels, and saw themselves as continuing a sacred tradition which linked them back to Solomon the Wise.

Solomon was known as the wise teacher speaker (Ecclesiastes 1:1), the Preacher, the son of King David who inherited the task to build a temple for the great war god of his ancestors (1 Kings 5:5).

Solomon lives on in his legends of magic, of wisdom and song, of compassion and healing, of astrology and his forbidden obsession with the god Baal and the goddess Asherah. Saint and heretic. Solomon is this pivotal character, riding two horses at the same time, knowledge of good and evil, sacred and profane, accepted and rejected, religion and magic.

The chief priests and scribes (Jewish leaders) were upset that Jesus was at the Jerusalem temple grounds and the people were calling him the son of David (Matthew 21:15). The blind call out to Jesus: compassionate son of David (Matthew 9:27). The people called Jesus son of David because he healed those in need (Matthew 12:23). Part of what Jesus heals is nothing to do with physical disease, but is rather to do with mental disease. How do you heal intolerance? How do you heal injustice? How do you heal persecution? How do you heal hate? How do you heal revenge? How do you heal terrorism?

Ecclesiastes 1:2 Vanity of vanities, saith the Preacher, vanity of vanities; all is vanity.

The Jesus question (Matthew 22:42-46; Mark 12:35-37): Is Christ the same as the son of David? Is the Messiah prophesized to come the same as Solomon returned? Are they in fact not the same, and not only not the same, but even being the exact opposites? Messiah expected is to be a war hero for the Jews, defeat the foreigners, and reestablish a pure homogeneous Israel. Solomon returned would be a wise speaker, a channel for the holy spirits of Baal and Asherah to play a mystical role once again in the lives of the people. Who is this rejected foundation, the son who thought outside of the box? Everything thought is turned upside down, the first becomes last while the last becomes first. The good are seen as hypocrites and the obviously different misfits are seen as saints. So little time, so much to unlearn. This lens will change the way you look at Jesus forever. You are forewarned.

Ignorance

Forbidden Knowledge

The Gnostics read the Jewish scriptures (the Bible) in an upside down way from how surviving Christianity views it. The God of the Bible was given the name Yaldabaoth in Gnostic texts and understood as a tyrant force that kept the people in fear and ignorance. For the Gnostics, there was a Higher God than Yaldabaoth. It may seem a radically different lens to look through, but for many early Christians this was the way they understood Christ: as the liberator from outdated traditions.

Yaldabaoth refused people knowing good from evil, refused people from trusting in their own wisdom (Genesis 3:5-6).

Genesis 2:17: But of the tree of the knowledge of good and evil, thou shalt not eat of it: for in the day that thou eatest thereof thou shalt surely die.

In Hebrew good is "towb" and evil is "rah". The Law of Moses is called the "to-rah", the official encoded list of 613 commandments. The rule book was defined by and controlled by a specially appointed priesthood. This lists what is forbidden and what is allowed, in actions and in thoughts and even in emotions. If you are going to set up a theocracy, the number one fear is what would happen if folks just did what they felt was right instead of obeying the rules out of fear? They can't be allowed to consider that they can think for themselves and know for themselves how to act and think and feel. What if they decide to hate what is supposed to be loved or dare to love what is supposed to be hated? What if they break rules and consider that there never should have been such silly rules in the first place? It would result in uncontrolled chaos, wouldn't it? Wouldn't it?

Genesis 3:1-5 Now the serpent was more subtil than any beast of the field which the Lord God had made. And he said unto the woman, Yea, hath God said, Ye shall not eat of every tree of the garden? And the woman said unto the serpent, We may eat of the fruit of the trees of the garden: But of the fruit of the tree which is in the midst of the garden, God hath said, Ye shall not eat of it, neither shall ye touch it, lest ye die. And the serpent said unto the woman, Ye shall not surely die: For God doth know that in the day ye eat thereof, then your eyes shall be opened, and ye shall be as gods, knowing good and evil.

The Apocryphon of John 22.3-9 shares: But what they call the tree of knowledge of good and evil, which is the Epinoia of the light, they stayed in front of it in order that he (Adam) might not look up to his fullness and recognize the nakedness of his shamefulness. But it was I (Christ) who brought about that they ate.

Epinoia means highest thought. While the lower god wanted to maintain his control, the higher light desired humanity to look up and to understand and to become spiritually mature. Epinoia is Holy Spirit, the Mother force, Wisdom.

The Apocryphon of John 23.26-35 continues: And through her they have tasted the perfect Knowledge. I appeared in the form of an eagle on the tree of knowledge, which is the Epinoia from the fore-knowledge of the pure light, that I might teach them and awaken them out of the depth of sleep. For they were both in a fallen state and they recognized their nakedness. The Epinoia appeared to them as a light and she awakened their thinking.

Through the "normal" lens of modern Christian understanding, the original people disobeyed God by listening to the Devil who appeared as a snake and tricked them into eating from the forbidden tree, thus introducing "original sin" into all of humanity ever since.

Through the "gnostic" lens, represented by the early Christian text, the Apocryphon of John, the original people were trapped in ignorance by the archons lead by Yaldabaoth and it was Christ who convinced them to partake of the symbolic forbidden fruit of Epinoia, the Divine Mother First Thought that exists above the gods (archons) and beyond our cosmos that is able to connect us and teach us and transform us – the Holy Spirit. In this version, the serpent was actually an eagle, a bird that can fly high and see far and thus understand better than one who is limited in place and vision.

Here we find the first example of when we read it upside down it makes much better sense, the first shall be last and the last shall be first. This is how the early Gnostic Christians read the Jewish scriptures, with the idea in mind that you can read it all inverted. Their Ultimate God is not the Ultimate God. The temptation is actually a spiritual awakening event. The banishment from the paradise of Eden is actually an escape from a mind controlled prison. So here we look through crazy backwards lens, which would actually seem quite normal had not the Catholic Christians persecuted and eliminated (or distorted) the traditions of the Gnostic Christians. Today, all modern Christianity variations, all the Protestant denominations, even non-denominational churches, are derived from the surviving Catholic anti-Gnostic tradition.

Identifying Iblis

Iblis is the devil in the Arabic Qur'an, a name similar to Diabolos in Greek, the word in the New Testament that is translated as "devil" in English. In Islamic thought, angels are created out of light and have no free will and cannot sin, but jinn (genies) are created out of fire and have free will and can choose to rebel against Allah. Iblis is a jinn (genie), identified with the tempting serpent in the Garden of Eden and with the Christian concept of a Satan who is purposed with leading humans astray from the straight and narrow path of God.

It is a very simple yet powerful story that works well for controlling the masses. Divide everything into God and Iblis, submitted and astray, saved and damned, truth and lies, and give this great dividing line a simple story, and what you get are otherwise intelligent and reasonable people fighting holy wars against those who are different because they can be labeled as being under the sway of Satan.

AL BAQARAH 2:34-36 When God created humanity, he commanded all the angels to bow down to his ultimate creation, but Iblis, being a jinn, refused to bow before people. So the forbidden tree of Eden was poisoned with harm and transgression. Iblis (Satan) tricked humanity into slipping from the perfect obedience of God and they were exiled from the peaceful garden into the world of peoples being divided and violent towards each other.

AL A'RAF 7:12 Iblis, being a jinn, had the free will thought that he was superior to humanity, for he was made of fire while people were made of dirt.

AL A'RAF 7:16-21 Iblis vows to stand by the "straight way" and assault humanity, tricking them to eat the forbidden fruit. God vows to fill hell with anyone who is persuaded by Iblis to rebel.

AL HIJR 15:39 Iblis proclaims that he will make wrong seem right.

TA HA 20:117 Adam was warned that Iblis the jinn refused to prostrate to Adam and that he had vowed to trick Adam into getting kicked out of the Garden to live in misery.

TA HA 20:120 Iblis presents his evil temptation to Adam, the Tree of Eternity, the kingdom that never decays. This detail is not clear in the existing Jewish texts of the Eden story, but as the finds of the Dead Sea Scrolls and Nag Hammadi Library teach us, there must have been a great deal of ancient texts forever lost for each one discovered preserved for future generations to rediscover. This thought of a sense of eternity along with a kingdom that can never fade plays right into the concepts of Jesus of eternal life and a kingdom not of this world.

AL ISRA 17:62-64 Iblis vows to hold humanity under his sway except for the few who are faithful to God. He tempts people with a seductive voice that makes the worst seem for the best, encouraging the most violent of assaults, lying promises of wealth and future lands for rich happy protected children to come.

So it is interesting to pause in consideration here. Who is Iblis in the Bible? Who encourages violence and promises promised lands? One thing Muhammad was certain of was that he needed his Qur'an to be pure because both the Jewish scriptures and Christian scriptures had been tampered with, distorted, that they contained errors and lies.

Job 2:3 And the LORD said unto Satan, Hast thou considered my servant Job, that *there is* none like him in the earth, a perfect and an upright man, one that feareth God, and escheweth evil? and still he holdeth fast his integrity, although thou movedst me against him, to destroy him without cause.

We have Yaldabaoth (the LORD) trying to destroy Job, Satan taunting that Job is only faithful when good things are happening to him. It is interesting in this text that Satan is tempting God who is curious about the reaction of the human.

In Islamic thought, everyone is assigned a jinn who whispers bad advice in the ear. AL MA'IDAH 5:90-91 lists out intoxicants, gambling, the dedication of stones, the divination of arrows as coming from Iblis. Are the stones the columns of Baal? AL NISA 4:116-117 states that those calling on a goddess are actually in communication with Iblis. The attributes of goddess spirituality are the love of nature, the sense that sexuality is spiritual (Venus, Aphrodite), that the mind can learn and master (Saraswati), and the body can excel in sports and arts (Minerva). This is the ancient Fundamentalist battle against people understanding and exercising their sense of free will. AL NISA 4:120 explains that Iblis fills minds with promises, false desires, deception, then the lost soul proceeds to follow this corruption and disobey and become arrogant and perverted.

AL NAML 27:17 Solomon ruled jinn and men and birds, fire and earth and wind. He was not afraid to rule in kingdoms not bound by the ground of earth. In Islamic legend, Solomon bound and controlled the magic of the jinn (genies).

Forbidden Interaction

He thrives on keeping humanity confused, separated by languages and groups so they will not work together (Genesis 11:7-8).

Mark 16:17 And these signs shall follow them that believe; in my name shall they cast out devils; they shall speak with new tongues;

Acts 2:4 And they were all filled with the Holy Ghost, and began to speak with other tongues, as the Spirit gave them utterance.

Acts 2:11 Cretes and Arabians, we do hear them speak in our tongues the wonderful works of God.

1 Corinthians 14:18 I thank my God, I speak with tongues more than ye all:

Revelation 7:9 After this I beheld, and, lo, a great multitude, which no man could number, of all nations, and kindreds, and people, and tongues, stood before the throne, and before the Lamb, clothed with white robes, and palms in their hands;

The communication barrier is broken by Jesus.

Yaldabaoth speaks only through Moses (Exodus 19:12-13) from the sacred mountain peak. Any other person or animal who dares to touch the mountain must be killed. Then, once the group became more nomadic, Yaldabaoth was carried in the Ark of the Covenant. Anyone coming near must die (Numbers 1:51). Anyone looking inside must die (Numbers 4:20).

Matthew 5:1 And seeing the multitudes, he went up into a mountain: and when he was set, his disciples came unto him:

No one dare to accompany the Law (Moses) or the Prophets (Elijah) as they ascended the mountain. Jesus invited the multitudes, anyone who wanted to listen, and anyone who wanted to be his disciple. And he encouraged them to own the truths and share them with the world. Broadcast to the whole world. No more forbidden secret controlled tradition.

Thomas 33 Jesus said, "Preach from your housetops that which you will hear in your ear. For no one lights a lamp and puts it under a bushel, nor does he put it in a hidden place, but rather he sets it on a lampstand so that everyone who enters and leaves will see its light."

John 7:35 Then said the Jews among themselves, Whither will he go, that we shall not find him? Will he go unto the dispersed among the Gentiles, and teach the Gentiles?

Jesus, as it turned out, was for the whole world except for the Jews, the complete mirror inverse of the Messiah. Jesus is not the completion of Judaism. He is the antidote. The Roman Empire was infected with the narrow minded violent xenophobic "good people" threatening the peace and cosmopolitan harmony. Jesus is the antibiotic for the Messianic faith infection.

The Lion

Apocryphon of John 9.25—10.19: "And the Sophia of the Epinoia, being an aeon, conceived a thought from herself and the conception of the invisible Spirit and foreknowledge. She wanted to bring forth a likeness out of herself without the consent of the Spirit, - he had not approved - and without her consort, and without his consideration. And though the person of her maleness had not approved, and she had not found her agreement, and she had thought without the consent of the Spirit and the knowledge of her agreement, (yet) she brought forth. And because of the invincible power which is in her, her thought did not remain idle, and something came out of her which was imperfect and different from her appearance, because she had created it without her consort. And it was dissimilar to the likeness of its mother, for it has another form. "And when she saw (the consequences of) her desire, it changed into a form of a lion-faced serpent. And its eyes were like lightning fires which flash. She cast it away from her, outside that place, that no one of the immortal ones might see it, for she had created it in ignorance. And she surrounded it with a luminous cloud, and she placed a throne in the middle of the cloud that no one might see it except the Holy Spirit who is called the mother of the living. And she called his name Yaldabaoth.

Yaldabaoth is Gnostic code word for there being a spiritual force in the cosmos like the Plato concept of the demiurge, the creative and controlling god in charge. In exploring the Jewish scriptures, the Lord God Almighty is labelled Yaldabaoth, which means childish ruler. The myth was woven that he was the son of the Sophia of the Epinoia, the mother wisdom of the highest consciousness, but missing the connection of having a father. He was thus incomplete, deficient, imperfect, and ignorant. It is this childish imperfect demanding god that arrives with a quest for control and absolute devotion.

Thomas 7 Jesus said, "Blessed is the lion which becomes man when consumed by man; and cursed is the man whom the lion consumes, and the lion becomes man."

There is a dualism of forces at play within each of us, the inflated ego lion and the potentially enlightened and wise human. If the wisdom part of us wins out, the lion is tamed and becomes a useful part of the human experience. If the beast part of us wins out, the lion is untamed and rules the human with passions for conquest and control. There is a counterpart in religion itself. The old god concept of war and riches and chosen people gets tamed by the new god concept of compassion and universality. The second century Christian teacher, Marcion, taught that Yaldabaoth the demiurge will be saved in the end. Ideas are possible through a Gnostic lens that would not make sense through the traditional Christian lens.

Exodus 3:14 And God said unto Moses, I AM THAT I AM: and he said, Thus shalt thou say unto the children of Israel, I AM hath sent me unto you.

"I am" in Greek is the word "ego". If Yaldabaoth is ego then is Baal the suppressed id (the heart)? It will be for Freud students to contemplate. The Kabbalah tree diagram shows a left hand path and a right hand path. Perhaps both are required?

Intolerance

Lies

The real visionaries of old were pursued with hatred, excluded as disreputable, remembered in "spin doctor" histories in bad terms, spoken of as having been bad people (Luke 6:22-23). It is because they followed the music of the son of man (Solomon) and had visions and became prophets of the sky (ouranos).

Jesus contrasts the real visionaries with the false prophets without true Gnosis (Luke 6:24-26) so respected and studied by the authorities on Judaism, the scribes and Pharisees, the Bible scholars. They valued their wealth, their comfort, their satisfaction, their happiness, and their legacies as being the good people, remembered for being saints.

Law | Torah (of Death)

Fundamentalist Christians believe the Bible is the answer, the word of God guide and directive. This becomes a problem if it is opened and the wrong verses are read. It can destroy peace, diversity, harmony, beauty, cooperation, compassion. All in the name of God. All in the name of mental projections of concepts that are identified as God's will.

The Law of Moses listed out those who must be killed for being different: homosexual men (Leviticus 20:13), mediums and psychics (Leviticus 20:27), dreamers and visionaries (Deuteronomy 13:6), anyone having sex with foreign women (Numbers 25:6-9), any girl having sex before marriage (Deuteronomy 22:20-21). Not just talked about in a derogatory fashion, not just harassed, the Law of Moses instructs the good people to go witch hunt crazy, create inquisitions, support crusades, and actually literally kill people in the name of God. Sadism and cruelty are praised and demanded by the Law of Moses.

It wasn't just a xenophobia of anyone and anything different or foreign, the Law divided the people of the world into those you love and those you hate, saved and damned, us and them. For living with the chosen saved people, do not kill, do not steal, and do not touch someone else's wife. For the damned hated people who are in the way of your taking over the Promised Land for yourselves, invade their towns, kill them all, take whatever you want, and you can keep their young virgin daughters for yourselves.

John 8:42-44 Jesus said unto them, If God were your Father, ye would love me: for I proceeded forth and came from God; neither came I of myself, but he sent me. Why do ye not understand my speech? Even because ye cannot hear my word. Ye are of your father the devil, and the lusts of your father ye will do. He was a murderer from the beginning, and abode not in the truth, because there is no truth in him. When he speaketh a lie, he speaketh of his own: for he is a liar, and the father of it.

There is a great disconnect between the Jesus "God" and the Torah "God". The Christian Gnostics did not think of Jesus as being a continuation of the Jewish traditions. When Marcion collected the Epistles of Paul and a Gospel, he didn't append these onto a collection of Jewish texts, as we now have it as "The Bible". There were centuries of editing texts, eliminating texts, and inventing texts all to support the new "catholic and apostolic" lens. The "Church Fathers" saw Jesus as the son of the Torah "God" and his role as being the Jewish Messiah has been postponed until he returns on the clouds. The "Church Fathers" hold the position that the Gnostic Christians edited out the parts that they didn't agree with. It is more likely that the Gnostics possessed earlier versions before very much editing had taken place. If we look through the Gnostic lens, Jesus is the antidote for the Torah "God", reaching beyond the cherished traditions to a "God is Love" that is above and beyond any previous human conception of God.

Thomas 17   Jesus said, "I shall give you what no eye has seen and what no ear has heard and what no hand has touched and what has never occurred to the human mind."

Luke 6:27-29 offers the concept that "goodness" does not come from defining "badness" and hating it. The self-righteous "good people" were very mean to those they did not agree with, did not understand, and did not allow to be different. True "goodness" comes with love for the hated, comfort for the violent, finding good qualities in people who only find bad qualities in you, having good wishes for those who insult you, offering peace in response to violence and charity in response to theft. Cosmopolitan love is a radically alien spiritual concept from the lens of the xenophobic violence, the two have danced in religion for ages and cultures to this day. Christianity grew in waves of both warrior crusaders and mystic monks.

Ancient Judaism was not just rallying support for the next violent revolution, it also sang Psalms, praised Wisdom, and formed peaceful contemplative communities such as that of the fabled Essenes. From the perspective of Jesus, his "God is Love" was squarely at odds with their "God is Victory" zealot blind faith that they could defeat the Roman Empire, but in agreement with the alternative Jewish concept of God shared by the Essenes.

Hate

Dead Sea Scrolls Community Rule 1QS 1:9-11   He is to teach them both to love all the Children of Light—each commensurate with his rightful place in the council of God—and to hate all the Children of Darkness, each commensurate with his guilt and the vengeance due him from God.

The distinction between neighbor and enemy, good and evil, light and darkness, was carried out to its practical conclusion of exercising love for the neighbor and hate for the enemy. It is this mindset that Jesus is questioning here: Matthew 5:43-44 Ye have heard that it hath been said, Thou shalt love thy neighbour, and hate thine enemy. But I say unto you, Love your enemies, bless them that curse you, do good to them that hate you, and pray for them which despitefully use you, and persecute you;

Threats | Fear

If you do not enforce these rules, Yaldabaoth will give you terror and fear and weakness, your enemies will eat all your food, defeat you, enslave you, and you will insanely run around aimlessly (Leviticus 26:16-17). Yaldabaoth will send wild animals to attack you and run away with your children, destroy all your cattle and leave you alone and deserted (Leviticus 26:22).

John 14:27 Peace I leave with you, my peace I give unto you: not as the world giveth, give I unto you. Let not your heart be troubled, neither let it be afraid.

The expectation was that everyone memorize the dogmatic assertions, everyone recite back without question. Questioning must result in the entire community gathering to stone the blasphemer to death (Leviticus 24:16). Complaining is offensive to Yaldabaoth. When his anger is aroused, fire will devour the area around the complainers (Numbers 11:1). Disobeying a priest or judge demands death so that the people will be afraid to think for themselves (Deuteronomy 17:12-13). No one expects the Spanish Inquisition.

John 10:31 Then the Jews took up stones again to stone him.

Being Exclusive

Exodus 20:3 Thou shalt have no other gods before me.

The Apocryphon of John 11:15-22 applies the Gnostic lens: "Now the archon who is weak has three names. The first name is Yaldabaoth, the second is Saklas, and the third is Samael. And he is impious in his arrogance which is in him. For he said, 'I am God and there is no other God beside me,' for he is ignorant of his strength, the place from which he had come.

Yaldabaoth, Saklas, and Samael: childish authority, foolish, and blind. It brings up a vision of a very powerful child king who rules with absolute power, but is impulsive, sending his troops to unwinnable battles, blind to the needs and problems facing the people around him. Samael is represented in the Talmud as the accuser and destroyer, both good and evil, a force of wrath and death and destruction.

Whoever quotes from another religion must die (Deuteronomy 18:20).

Exodus 22:19 records the ancient Law as demanding that anyone who is observed to partake of any other religion must die. The Bible records they were very serious about this commandment. Exodus 32:25-29 has Moses and the Levites convincing the people that it was the will of God to pick up swords and to go into the campsite and kill relatives, friends, and neighbors. This was so that God could consecrate and bless them. Three thousand people were slaughtered that day.

If a close member of your family mentions any other religion, you are commanded to stone him to death (Deuteronomy 13:7-12). Matthew 10:21-23 has Jesus lamenting: Brother against brother, parent against child, child against parent, without mercy or hesitation, violent to the death. They will hate you if you follow me. Who is devoted to the end will find an end to suffering (sozo in Greek). The end of suffering is a Buddhist concept. The way that the Gospel works is that it is a commentary on Jewish scripture, pesher style like seen in the Dead Sea Scrolls. The words that sound so obscure are cutting and illuminating once you understand what they are standing up against, once you learn the keys, the references. But sadly none of that is taught or considered important. The "Bible in a bubble" cannot be properly understood. So much of the context was destroyed or forgotten.

If you discover a town where they mention other religions, you must kill everyone there with swords, pile up everything they owned and burn it all in a great fire (Deuteronomy 13:13-17).

Jesus teaches Buddhist and Stoic ideas and actually criticizes and corrects ideas from Judaism. He was the ultimate heretic. They didn't collect the best ideas from the Torah and have Jesus teach the Law to the Jews of his day, much less to the world beyond. The teachings of Jesus either criticize the Law or discuss ideas in multiple foreign ways. He teaches by fables like Aesop, Pythagorean ascetics, Stoic detachment, and Buddhist compassion.

Find everyone who has committed themselves to another god, identify their leaders, cut off their heads and line them up in the sun (Numbers 25:4-5).

John 19:7 The Jews answered him, We have a law, and by our law he ought to die, because he made himself the Son of God.

Jesus is in contradiction to the Torah, the Law, the tradition that demands judgment and death, division and xenophobia. He is both critic and victim.

Promised Land Manifest Destiny

Deuteronomy 32:23-27 paints the picture: Yaldabaoth will throw disasters, endless shooting arrows, hunger, plague, scourge, wild animals with fangs, poisonous snakes. Outside will be sword fights. Inside will be terror. Boys and girls die with babies and old people, crushed into the dust, their history erased and forgotten.

So which are the good guys and which are the bad guys? You'd think you could judge the trees by their fruit (Matthew 7:16). The mad terrorists raping and pillaging are the prophets and saints and crusaders, the supposed good guys. The being different and separate "peace and love" types, from the ancient people of Baal to the Gnostics and Cathars, the supposed bad guys. But good and bad are just according to which lens you happen to be looking through.

The thing about journeying to your promised land is that there are already other people living there. The thing about your people having a manifest destiny to inherit the earth is that there are already other people living there. Combine these thoughts with a fear driven intolerance of anyone and anything different and the result was very violent and destructive. Repeatedly. In many lands and many ages. To today.

Considering the people already living in the Promised Land, they are cursed for destruction, every one of their towns (Deuteronomy 3:6-7). The Law of Yaldabaoth demands you kill every man, woman, and child, but you can keep the livestock and any of their valuables. Now go! Yaldabaoth will make it to where you can conquer your promised land (Deuteronomy 7:2-3). Your role in this is to curse them all to utter destruction. You must not make a peace treaty. You must not show any mercy. You must not even spare their women to marry. You must not collect any of their religious ideas (Deuteronomy 12:2-3). You must completely destroy every sacred site, tear down their altars, smash their sacred stones, burn their sacred poles, and smash their statues. Erase all memory of their gods.

In all practicality, the Law was revised a bit: When you arrive at a town, if they refuse to accept the terms that you now own all of their property and they are now your slaves, you must kill every man, but keep the women and children and livestock and valuables for yourselves (Deuteronomy 20:10-14).

Now if the Bible is your word of God handbook for life, what can verses like these inspire? Christianity destroyed libraries and persecuted other religions into oblivion: the Orphic Mysteries, the Manichaeans, and the Cathars. The same inspiration gave rights to the Conquistadors to take over and the United States to run amuck with its Manifest Destiny.

Words like genocide and holocaust and terrorism evoke strong emotional responses. If in modern times we encountered a story of an invasion resulting in every last person in the invaded territory being killed, everything being destroyed completely, without a sole survivor (Joshua 11:14), the response would be outrage at the invaders. There is some strange lens through which Fundamentalist Christians look through at the stories of the chosen people being helped by God to inherit their promised land.

Jesus taught to love your enemies, even those persecuting you. This was in exact contradiction to the dictates of the Law of Moses. This is a stance against the nature and purpose of the Messiah, the Christ, war hero to exterminate the oppressors of the chosen people and establish a kingdom that can never be conquered. Jesus was not only not that, he was the anti-that. He's not ever coming back to become that which he back then opposed. Jesus was the antidote for Simon bar Kokhba. Do we dare say the phrase "anti-Christ" as a term to describe Jesus? Through this lens, it seems appropriate.

Messiah

John 17:14 I have given them thy word; and the world hath hated them, because they are not of the world, even as I am not of the world.

John 18:36 Jesus answered, My kingdom is not of this world: if my kingdom were of this world, then would my servants fight, that I should not be delivered to the Jews: but now is my kingdom not from hence.

Jesus is not the Messiah. The Messiah's kingdom was definitely of this world, a kingdom of Jews, a kingdom that could defeat all who stood in the way of establishing a theocracy based in Jerusalem. The Messiah expected to appear was a warrior hero exclusively for the Jews.

Jesus is presented as not fighting any earthly land battle for promised lands, but if he were a revolutionary leader, he would not have fought on the side of the Jews, and the Jews would want him captured as their enemy. The ascetic sense of being detached from this world and its politics and wars and being focused on a higher reality places Jesus at odds with the very definition of the Messiah as predicted by the Jewish Prophets. It must have been amusing and confusing for Christians to have asked the Jews for centuries why they didn't believe Jesus was the Messiah. Uh, because we are in persecuted exile from Jerusalem and do not live in an unconquerable kingdom ruled by the Messiah there. Very simple bottom line definition for Jews. Fundamentalist Christians imagine Jesus returning from the sky to start a violent Armageddon world war destruction like we have never experienced before. Hmm.

Revelation 16:16 And he gathered them together into a place called in the Hebrew tongue Armageddon.

First Enoch explains the "righteous and elect one", the Messiah, comes in the spirit of violent opposition to the crimes of humanity, defeating the foreign rulers, such as Caesar in Rome. The one definite mark of the real Messiah would have been the violent defeat of the Roman Empire. This is what the Romans needed a solution for.

1 Enoch 53:1-7 My eyes saw there a deep valley with a wide mouth. And all those who dwell upon the earth, the sea, and the islands shall bring to it gifts, presents, and tributes; yet this deep valley shall not become full. They shall fulfill the criminal deeds of their hands and eat all the produce of crime which the sinners toil for. Sinners shall be destroyed from before the face of the Lord of the Spirits – they shall perish eternally, standing before the face of his earth. So I saw all the angels of plague co-operating and preparing all the chains of Satan. And I asked the angel of peace, who was going with

me, "For whom are they preparing these chains?" And he answered me, saying, "They are preparing these for the kings and the potentates of this earth in order that they may be destroyed thereby. After this, the Righteous and Elect One will reveal the house of his congregation. From that time, they shall not be hindered in the name of the Lord of the Spirits. And these mountains shall become flat like earth in the presence of his righteousness, and the hills shall become like a fountain of water. And the righteous ones shall have rest from the oppression of sinners."

Dead Sea Scrolls 4Q285 Frag 5 The king of the Kittim (Caesar) will stand in the judgment when the Leader of the people, the Branch of David, will sentence him to death.

Dead Sea Scrolls 4Q252 5.1-4 A ruler shall not depart from the tribe of Judah when Israel has dominion. And the one who sits on the throne of David shall never be cut off, because the "ruler's staff" is the covenant of the kingdom, and the thousands of Israel are "the feet," until the Righteous Messiah, the Branch of David, is come. For to him and to his seed the covenant of the kingdom of His people has been given for the eternal generations.

Luke 21:24 And they shall fall by the edge of the sword, and shall be led away captive into all nations: and Jerusalem shall be trodden down of the Gentiles, until the times of the Gentiles be fulfilled.

This sounds like the events of 135, after the fall of the office of the high priest Eleazar [Lazarus] and the messiah Simon bar Kokhba. After this time the Jews were forbidden to return to Jerusalem. Jesus didn't fly out of the sky to save them.

It is interesting that the type of anti-Messiah Messiah that Jesus is presented as being is expressed in the Dead Sea Scrolls. It is also interesting that it is only preserved in scraps of fragments and that the original keepers of the archeological find limited access and forbid publication after the discovery in 1956. Conspiracy theory?

Dead Sea Scrolls 4Q521 Frag 2 and Frag 4 Col 2 For the heavens and the earth shall listen to His Messiah and all which is in them shall not turn away from the commandments of the holy ones. Strengthen yourselves, O you who seek the Lord, in His service. Will you not find the Lord in this, all those who hope in their heart? For the Lord seeks the pious and calls the righteous by name. Over the humble His spirit hovers, and He renews the faithful in His strength. For He will honor the pious upon the throne of His eternal kingdom, setting prisoners free, opening the eyes of the blind, raising up those who are bowed down...and the Lord shall do glorious things which have not been done, just as He said. For He shall heal the critically wounded. He shall revive the dead, He shall send good news to the afflicted.

In 4Q521 we get a window into a different expectation for the Messiah, one more Jesus like. Everyone was not a war-monger. Some Jews were true visionaries. The pacifists were persecuted, labeled as traitors, unpatriotic, lacking in faith, weak cowards.

Jesus 2.0

Thomas 19 Jesus said, "Blessed is he who came into being before he came into being. If you become my disciples and listen to my words, these stones will minister to you. For there are five trees for you in Paradise which remain undisturbed summer and winter and whose leaves do not fall. Whoever becomes acquainted with them will not experience death."

The "five trees" of Joshua 10:26 were for killing the enemies of Joshua, which was the same name as Jesus in the Greek LXX version. The new Joshua/Jesus offers five trees which will guarantee not facing death. In the verses that follow in Joshua chapters 10 and 11, a great deal of violence, death, and destruction followed. Traditions about early Christians have them avoiding the Jewish revolutionary conflicts both in 70 and in 135. Eusebius records the tradition that the early Christians were warned in a vision to flee to Pella to avoid the coming war and destruction of the Temple in Jerusalem (Eusebius: History of the Church book 3: chapter 5). In the Simon bar Kokhba revolt that lasted from 132 to 135, Christians were said to not have been supporting Simon as being the Messiah who was prophesized to save the Jewish people from the Romans. The contrast between war and peace, death and life, destruction and resurrection, plays out vividly in the Jesus traditions. The stones will serve the people of the new Joshua/Jesus, while the stones killed the people surrounding the old Joshua/Jesus. The remaining stone set in place by the old Joshua/Jesus is contrasted with the stone that has been miraculously rolled away in the presence of the new Joshua/Jesus (Matthew 28:2).

Joshua 10:26-27 And afterward Joshua smote them, and slew them, and hanged them on five trees: and they were hanging upon the trees until the evening. And it came to pass at the time of the going down of the sun, that Joshua commanded, and they took them down off the trees, and cast them into the cave wherein they had been hid, and laid great stones in the cave's mouth, which remain until this very day.

Once again, the Jesus story is an antithesis, a literary antidote to the Messianic poison that had created so much violence and destruction.

Jewish Violent Revolutionaries

The Maccabees frame the ancient Jewish story of fighting outside influence, in their case the Greeks, and working with a vision of refocusing Judaism. It is their story that inspires the Hanukkah celebration to this day. Enter the Roman Empire into the refocused Jerusalem and these old success stories inspired faith in new violence, new rebellion, and new acts of terrorism against the foreigners who dared claim to control the Chosen People. The idea was that if they had enough faith that God would send the promised Messiah to help them win against any odds, including that of taking on the Roman Empire.

Josephus: The Wars of the Jews, Book 2, Chapter 3, tells of the Pentecost uprising of the Jewish terrorists who take control of Jerusalem in the year 66.

Josephus: The Wars of the Jews, Book 2, Chapter 8, Paragraph 1 in part: A certain Galilean, whose name was Judas, prevailed with his countrymen to revolt; and said they were cowards if they would endure to pay a tax to the Romans, and would, after God, submit to mortal men as their lords. This man was a teacher of a peculiar sect of his own, and was not at all like the rest of those their leaders.

It is always some cult leader who makes a stand and you may think he represents his religion, but he is just a nobody that somehow has gotten the attention of enough supporters to be dangerous.

Matthew 22:17-21 Tell us therefore, What thinkest thou? Is it lawful to give tribute unto Caesar, or not? But Jesus perceived their wickedness, and said, Why tempt ye me, ye hypocrites? Shew me the tribute money. And they brought unto him a penny. And he said unto them, Whose is this image and superscription? They say unto him, Caesar's. Then saith he unto them, Render therefore unto Caesar the things which are Caesar's; and unto God the things that are God's.

Josephus: The Wars of the Jews, Book 2, Chapter 13, Paragraph 3 in part: There sprang up another sort of robbers in Jerusalem, which were called Sicarii, who slew men in the daytime, and in the midst of the city; this they did chiefly at the festivals, when they mingled themselves among the multitude, and concealed daggers under their garments, with which they stabbed those that were their enemies.

Josephus: The Wars of the Jews, Book 4, Chapter 4, Paragraph 3 in part: They are robbers, who by their prodigious wickedness have profaned the sacred floor, and who are in the now seen drinking themselves drunk in the sanctuary, and expending the spoils of those whom they have slaughtered upon their unsatiable bellies.

Matthew 26:52 Then said Jesus unto him, Put up again thy sword into his place: for all they that take the sword shall perish with the sword.

This is not something you'd ever quote the Messiah as saying to his faithful supporting warrior heroes.

Morning Star

AL TARIQ, the Night Star, is a surah (chapter) in the Qur'an. The Morning Star is presented as a bright protector (AL TARIQ 86:3-4) and as the Word that distinguishes Good from Evil (AL TARIQ 86:13).

Christianity was born out of Judaism during the age of failed Jewish revolutions against Roman rule. When Simon bar Kokhba was defeated by the Romans in the year 135, Hadrian set up a statue of Zeus (the abomination referred to in Mark 13:14 according to Jerome) on the site of the Temple, renamed the city and the region, exiling all Jews, forbidding their return. The Jerusalem promised by their scriptures, the Promised Land for the chosen people, was lost to them. Simon named himself Kokhba, meaning star, after the prophecy of a star appearing to save the people (Numbers 24:17). This set the stage for the now legendary Jesus to be defined as the Morning Star, but for his kingdom to conquer to be not of this world.

From a bigger perspective than that of the ancient Jews in Palestine, the other traditions were not destroyed, the religions, the philosophies, the myths, the legends, the pantheons of gods and goddesses, the poetic dramas, the statues and symbols, celebration events and rituals. We can use them to reconstruct windows back into the age when Christianity was created, when "Jesus" first appeared, when the Gnostics defined Christianity, before the Catholic "church fathers" poured the concrete that gelled him into the form of Christianity that dominates to this day.

David and Bathsheba

We can't understand who Jesus is without asking "who is Solomon?" We can't understand Solomon apart from the foundational story of his parents and his birth as preserved in 2 Samuel chapters 11 and 12.

David inherited the tradition of Exclusive Monotheism, he represented it well, the ordained face for his faith, the king resting on the victories of all those who had come before to conquer the Promised Land for the chosen people. He was the Messiah ("Anointed" one in charge), the Pope, the famous king David, the "bring out the harps and sing the Psalms" king David, God's own son on the throne ruling over God's own people in God's own land.

2 Samuel 11:11 tells the story of Uriah, the husband of Bathsheba, who refused to sleep with her on the grounds that he was camping with his troops, his knights, his terrorist army, who carried with them the sacred "Ark of the Covenant", the home and presence of the one and only true supreme God, and because of that he could not disqualify himself by having sexual relations, even with his own wife.

Bathsheba was the living embodiment of the "forbidden fruit" for King David. In Jewish legends she was the great granddaughter of the great visionary astrologer who had foreseen the destiny of her and her child as pivotal in changing the course of human history itself. She was the "Babylon" goddess, the sexual poison to his celibate admiring "sacred Ark" God Almighty.

The first child of David and Bathsheba died, being cursed by Nathan the Jewish prophet, only living for one week. The second birth was to be most magical and wise. He had two names, Solomon which means "of the sun", and Jedidiah which means "the love of Yah" (Yaldabaoth). It was his Solomon name, from his mother Bathsheba, which he would use when he became king. Solomon Jedidiah had two faces, two ways of thinking, and two worlds. Would he continue in his father's religion and tradition or would he follow his mother's enchantment? There were two roads that he could go by and which would his heart lead him towards?

Josephus: The Antiquities of the Jews, Book 8, Chapter 2, Paragraph 5 in part: Now the sagacity and wisdom which God had bestowed upon Solomon was so great, that he exceeded the ancients, insomuch that he was no way inferior to the Egyptians, who are said to have been beyond all men in understanding: nay, indeed, it is evident that their sagacity was very much inferior to that of the king's. He also excelled and distinguished himself in wisdom above those who were most eminent among the Hebrews at that time for shrewdness. [...] God also enabled him to learn that skill which excels demons, which is a science useful and sanative to men. He composed such incantations also by which distempers are alleviated. And he left behind him the manner of using exorcisms, by which they drive away demons, so that they never return.

Immediately after Solomon Jedidiah's birth, King David won an epic battle for the conquest of a city his troops had invaded and devastated.   He gathered all that was of value and made the surviving people to become his slaves. Among the spoils he discovered a majestic crown on the head of the forbidden idol representing the god Milcom and placed it on his own head. This is also symbolic of the loss of pure orthodox focus upon Yah (Yaldabaoth) alone. He had embraced the woman and he had put on the crown. Milcom is just another name for Baal.

2 Samuel 12:31 And he brought forth the people that were therein, and put them under saws, and under harrows of iron, and under axes of iron, and made them pass through the brickkiln: and thus did he unto all the cities of the children of Ammon. So David and all the people returned unto Jerusalem.

This is also 1 Chronicles 20:3. Just after Solomon was born, David defeats a king, takes all of his wealth, and enslaves all of his people.

The Goddess and the Ancient One

There are archetypes across the ancient world, ideas that arise around the world as if fueled by some morphic field driven by a cosmic desire to wake us up and gather us together. Looking at Judaism from the Greek (Roman) perspective, Yaldabaoth is like Ares (Mars), the god of conquest who lives for the defeat of enemies, ruling in fear, enforcing his will, being strong. Ares is unbalanced, destructive, and it was thought that there must be a counterpart, and that was Love,

Aphrodite. The Romans so loved the concept that they invented love stories for Venus (Aphrodite) and Mars (Ares). There is this vacuum in Judaism, this Mars without his Venus, this lone god without a goddess. The softer side of Jewish writings began filling the space with the idea that there is a "presence" of the god that is a female idea, the Shekinah. This "almost goddess" Jewish concept became thought of as Lady Wisdom, CHoKMaH in Hebrew, Sophia in Greek. This Wisdom "mother" to those who seek to be wise is the link back to the timeless past and future, beyond all, consuming all, watching all, ancient eternal knowledge. This god before time is Cronus in Greek, Saturn in the Roman world. Saturn, the Ancient One, was known in ancient Palestine as Chiun (Amos 5:26). Not only is there is a missing goddess factor in the Jewish concept of god. The Jewish god is a war god and there is a god above and beyond all the war gods, the God above God, the God before God.

The Forbidden Reflection

The pattern of night and day is so basic and so observed by everyone that it drives very ancient and deep set myths. The sun is the source for light during the day, but at night the sky is dark and the light is scattered into countless stars, wandering stars (planets), and the moon. The Morning Star, the planet Venus observed just before dawn, appears low in the sky, like a herald announcing the soon arrival of the sun god, the resurrection of the day and the end of the night. The crescent moon acts like a pointer to the sunrise. From thousands of years before Islam adopted the symbol of crescent moon and (wandering) star, the symbols were used by the Moabites, the Sumerians, and the Parthians.

The star part of the symbol is identified as being the wandering star, Venus. This is associated with Inanna, Astarte for the Greeks, Ishtar for the Assyrians, and Ashtoreth for the Phoenicians, who becomes the arch-nemesis of the Yaldabaoth story as told through the lens of Jewish scriptures. 1 Kings 11:33 and 2 Kings 23:13, for examples, point out that the people had forsaken the Yaldabaoth religion and become devoted to Ashtoreth.

The Presence

Jerome Commentary on the Bible: On Matthew 24.15   So when you see the standing in the holy place the abomination that causes desolation: or to the statue of the mounted Hadrian, which stands to this very day on the site of the Holy of Holies.

With the sacred site profaned, the magic was supposed to be stopped, the god could no longer be present. Hadrian knew that until the sacred site was profaned, the Jews would continue to rally enough blind faith to form new rebellions. Kittim war results: Caesar won, Zealots lost. Fast forward and how many crusading knights were sent from Europe to Jerusalem? Christianity had missed the very point of Jesus.

Just as Yaldabaoth was thought to be present in the holy of holies room in the Jerusalem temple, so too the ancient sites devoted to Ashtoreth became the sacred locations for the higher god, Chemosh according to the Moabites, Moloch according to the Ammonites and Phoenicians, Saturn, Baal-peop, Baal-zebub.

King David is the ancient Jewish legendary king like king Uther Pendragon is to the Camelot stories. Yaldabaoth had succeeded in inspiring the faithful to conquer the Promised Land and rally around his sacred anointed king who built him a temple in Jerusalem, a place for his presence, a symbol of his victory. As Uther's son, Arthur, changes Camelot after Uther's death, so does David's son, Solomon, change Palestine after David's death.

1 Kings 11:7 introduces the main plot of the story for this lens into what Jesus means and matters. Solomon is the son of King David, the next in line to lead the people of Yaldabaoth, said to be the wisest man who ever lived. Wise king Solomon dedicated a mountain in Jerusalem, the Mount of Olives that serves as the backdrop to much of the Gospel story, to Baal, to what was being pointed to by the Morning Star. All the work of Solomon was destroyed by a future king, Josiah (2 Kings 23:13-14). The sacred sites were destroyed. The sacred people were killed.

Zechariah 14:3-4 sets Yaldabaoth at war with the sacred mountain in view of his temple in Jerusalem. The Mount of Olives broken, leveled into a valley, according to this ancient Jewish prophet. And yet, centuries later we find Jesus sitting on the Mount of Olives teaching. The prophecy of Zechariah of the symbolic breaking of the symbol of Baal had failed. This was in the context of the invasion of foreign forces in Jerusalem (Zachariah 14:1-2), setting the context for God (acting through his Messiah) to reclaim Jerusalem. Matthew 24:3 has him ask the Gnostic question: When will the current aeon (world) end? Aeon is translated as world, but it really means age, dynasty of influence, period in history. When does what end? Jesus spoke in the temple, but lived on the Mount of Olives (Luke 21:37, Luke 22:39, John 8:1). In the final scenes of the Gospel, Jesus appears to his disciples, not in the temple, but on one of the sacred mountains. Why? There is a sermon on the mount, not a sermon in the temple. Why?

Mark 11:1 And when they came nigh to Jerusalem, unto Bethphage and Bethany, at the mount of Olives, he sendeth forth two of his disciples,

Luke 21:37 And in the day time he was teaching in the temple; and at night he went out, and abode in the mount that is called the mount of Olives.

Luke 22:39 And he came out, and went, as he was wont, to the mount of Olives; and his disciples also followed him.

Matthew 28:16 Then the eleven disciples went away into Galilee, into a mountain where Jesus had appointed them.

The ideal for a site sacred to Baal and Ashtoreth was a mountain setting, removed from the crowds and politics and religious controllers. There would be an altar for Baal, a symbol to gather around, like the way the staff of Dionysus was described. Baal is the connection point between the sacred world and the human world. Surrounding the symbol for Baal was a grove of trees planted. Fast forward centuries and people gather around the symbol of the Christian cross and decorate Christmas with trees. The grove of trees symbolized the presence of the goddess Ashtoreth.

The presence of the sacred sites demanded that the good people raid them, knock down the symbol of Baal and cut down all the trees of Ashtoreth, then sacrifice a bull to Yaldabaoth (Judges 6:28). Needless to say, the people didn't appreciate the acts of God-sponsored terrorism (Judges 6:30).

Matthew 23:29-31 Woe unto you, scribes and Pharisees, hypocrites! Because ye build the tombs of the prophets, and garnish the sepulchers of the righteous, and say, If we had been in the days of our fathers, we would not have been partakers with them in the blood of the prophets. Therefore ye be witnesses unto yourselves, that ye are the children of them which killed the prophets.

That is a very heavy thing for Jesus to have said to the scholarly representatives of Judaism: You are representing a tradition that murdered holy people.

The Pharisees identified with ancient Judaism, with the Jewish prophets, with those who represented Yaldabaoth in their violence against those who represented Baal. It would be like someone today judging a person who said they were Catholic by stating: O, so you represent the tradition that sent crusaders to murder the Cathars?

The ancient site of the Mount of Olives was just the tip of the iceberg. The story of Mount Carmel (1 Kings 18:18) plots the famous prophet Elijah against 450 priests of Baal and 400 priestesses of Ashtoreth. Yaldabaoth is on his side and he manages to kill them all (1 Kings 18:40).

Matthew 7:15 Beware of false prophets, which come to you in sheep's clothing, but inwardly they are ravening wolves.

Luke 6:44 For every tree is known by his own fruit. For of thorns men do not gather figs, nor of a bramble bush gather they grapes.

Matthew 23:27 Woe unto you, scribes and Pharisees, hypocrites! for ye are like unto whited sepulchres, which indeed appear beautiful outward, but are within full of dead men's bones, and of all uncleanness.

In spite of the efforts of Elijah and other Yaldabaoth fanatics, king after king of ancient Israel chose Baal and Ashtoreth instead of Yaldabaoth (1 Kings 22:51-53). Then king after king would become zealous of the Elijah faith and order further murder and destruction of the "alternative sacred". 2 Kings 10:18-28 has King Jehu tricking the prophets of Baal into gathering for a convention where he trapped them and killed them all. All their sacred art was gathered and burned. Their sacred house was completely destroyed. Mattan the high priest of Baal was murdered in front of his altar, his altar and art work destroyed (2 Kings 11:18). This may be complete fiction, but it inspired the Maccabees, the Zealots, the Simon bar Kokhba revolt, and other Jewish violent outbreaks. It seems the priests of Baal were the prototype for the persecuted heretics of Christian history, like the Cathars, the victims of the infamous witch hunts, and even down to the suppressed Native Americans.

AL SAFFAT 37:123-128 So also was Elias among those sent (by Us). Behold, he said to his people, "Will ye not fear (Allah)? Will ye call upon Ba'l and forsake the best of Creators – Allah, your Lord and Cherisher and the Lord and Cherisher of your fathers of old?" But they rejected him, and they will certainly be called up (for punishment) except the sincere and devoted servants of Allah (among them).

Astrology: Venus

When they say that ancient people "worshipped the host of heaven" as in 2 Kings 21:3, we shouldn't imagine the people thousands of years ago as being that much different from us. Stars and wandering stars (planets) and the shifting patterns of the ages could teach us about ourselves and about what changes are coming. There are twelve sets of stars forming the zodiac. In looking toward the sunrise just before dawn at the first day of spring, we look into a different "sign" than they looked at a couple thousand years ago. Where we see Aquarius dawning, at the time Christianity was forming, they saw Pisces dawning. Thus the fish symbol for early Christianity.

The star in the East, Matthew 2:2, that announces the birth of the new age, the new god, is Venus, the Morning Star.

May the Morning Star arise in your hearts, preaches St. Peter of old (1 Peter 1:19). What is different about planets (the word means wanderer) is that they are more dynamic than the fixed stars who only slowly move according to the time of year and the current age. The Morning Star is sacred and dynamic and linked with Jesus. Venus is interesting to watch, always low and near the horizon, never way up to where you have to bend your neck too far. As if she is hanging down near us with a purpose, comforting our transitions between light and darkness.

Christian tradition is a bit dyslexic on the topic because they insisted that the Gospel be appended onto the Jewish scriptures as a continuation and that Jesus is the Messiah, son of Yaldabaoth. All of the early Morning Star references had to be downplayed. The Roman god associated with the Morning Star, Lucifer, is to this day symbolic with "evil" and "the devil". As we have seen, "evil" and "devil" are just code for alternative and different. How alternative and different is Jesus? The simple herald of a new coming dawn that will replace the old aeon, the old order, with a new one is the greatest fear of those who want to maintain their control. "The first shall be last and the last shall be first" is not comforting to those on the top. Aster is Greek for star, as in Ashtoreth the goddess of the groves from ancient times. I wonder if the staff of Baal may have been used to align the viewing of the pre-dawn sky, focused upon the Morning Star awaiting the sunrise.

Revelation 2:28 introduces Jesus as the Morning Star. This is a very important key. Revelation 8:10-11 paints the scene with a bright star falling from heaven with wormwood, the bitter healing herb with magical properties. The fallen star, Revelation 9:1, is given the key to the abussos (bottomless pit, abyss, immeasurable depth), the cosmos. Christ is the fallen star descended with the healing medicine for the cosmos.

Absinthe, a liquor made with wormwood, is legendary for producing visions. It inspired the artist Vincent van Gogh.

Revelation 22:16 calls Jesus the Morning Star of David. Why of David? Solomon, a son of David, dedicated a lot of sacred sites to Baal and Ashtoreth (1 Kings 11:7). David's family knew the key was this "alien star god connection" to something from beyond that made the primitive religion of his warrior ancestors no longer have his spiritual focus and attention. This "pagan" forbidden influence was the pinch of yeast in the dough that changed kosher unleavened bread into a large fluffy loaf (Matthew 13:33).

Resurrecting the Goddess

The idea of a benevolent Mother figure, as the surviving images of Asherah appear, is so deeply rooted in human nature that no matter how violently it is suppressed, it will reappear. The vacuum was so strong in Christianity that mother Mary took over the symbology. The statues of mother Isis and baby Horus were relabeled as mother Mary and baby Jesus. In the Bible centered Protestant Christian world, Mary was dropped out of having a significant role in the religion. Gnostic texts are explicit about the Holy Spirit being the Mother, but this connection is unknown by most modern Christians. Lost is Lady Wisdom (Sophia), the role of Mary Magdalene, and the early Gnostic Christian love for enlightened women teachers.

Philip 55.23-28 Some said, "Mary conceived by the holy spirit." They are in error. They do not know what they are saying. When did a woman ever conceive by a woman?

Filtered through the misogynist church fathers, to this day the "Holy Spirit" is thought of as genderless and not as the Mother.

Lazarus / Asherah

Mary Magdalene, the anointer of Jesus, was concerned for her dying brother, Lazarus.

John 11:2 (It was that Mary which anointed the Lord with ointment, and wiped his feet with her hair, whose brother Lazarus was sick.)

The story is about having to enter the world of the Jews that wanted to kill Jesus in order to locate and resurrect the dead Lazarus.

John 11:43-44 And when he thus had spoken, he cried with a loud voice, Lazarus, come forth. And he that was dead came forth, bound hand and foot with graveclothes: and his face was bound about with a napkin. Jesus saith unto them, Loose him, and let him go.

The story takes on a different meaning when looked at through our Baal lens. The reviving of Lazarus is the revival of the Asherah tradition. The names are so close, the equation does not take much imagination to see: Asherah = Lazarus. How can a tradition so long dead be brought back to life? Can we venture into the violent chaos world of Zealot Judaism and revive the sacred Goddess from their repressed traditions? She is symbolically dead, hidden, bound. A new day is come where she is free to live again. The old order that so violently suppressed her is rapidly fading.

(Symbolic) Baptism of Fire

When most all you know about a people is from the propaganda of the writings of those that hated them and want you to also hate them, you have to read a bit between the lines of what is said. Until the rediscovery of the Nag Hammadi Library in 1945, all that was known about the early Christian Gnostics came from ancient writers that wanted to make them look bad and stupid.

2 Kings 21:6 and other Bible verses speak of pushing children into fire. Genesis 22:4-10 tells the story of Abraham offering his miracle son to die on the third day. Then at the last moment, as Abraham holds the knife ready to murder his child, he comes across an animal to sacrifice instead and takes it as a sign from God (Genesis 22:13). Through the traditional lens of Christianity, God goes

through with having his only son killed, but he was revived on the third day. Life and death present a very basic thought subject which has been considered in myth and philosophy and poetry for as long as people have been able to think. Apart from looking through the lens of Bible scholars, there is no evidence in the study of the ancient world that devotees to Baal (or any variations thereof) would ritually murder their children in sacred fires. The ancient Mystery plays dealt with death and rebirth, acted out in scenes, symbolized in rituals and the partaking of chemical inspirations, but the Mystery plays actually killed no one, and actually brought no one back to life in a literal sense.

Dead Sea Scrolls Thanksgiving Scroll 1QH 13:7-9 You sent me to live with a crowd of fishermen. They cast their net onto the water and hunt for the wicked. You set me there to judge, making strong the wisdom of truth in my heart, giving the flowing stream of the Testament for all who desire it.

This text, preserved better than others of the Dead Sea Scrolls, could have been the inspiration for Jesus to begin his ministry by befriending fishermen. The theme of the document is that of a Servant being inspired by the Holy Spirit of the Lord. [Dead Sea Scrolls Thanksgiving Scroll 1QH 4:26] This Servant (Messiah) is the leader of the Poor, the people of the "New" Testament. The prophecy continues that not only will the Poor experience God-sent miracles, the Servant will be baptized with fire, refined seven times like silver by a silversmith. [Dead Sea Scrolls Thanksgiving Scroll 1QH 13:15-16]

Mark 9:49-50 For every one shall be salted with fire, and every sacrifice shall be salted with salt. Salt is good: but if the salt have lost his saltness, wherewith will ye season it? Have salt in yourselves, and have peace one with another.

1 Corinthians 3:13-14 Every man's work shall be made manifest: for the day shall declare it, because it shall be revealed by fire; and the fire shall try every man's work of what sort it is. If any man's work abide which he hath built thereupon, he shall receive a reward.

We can see the symbology here. We understand that early Christians were not literally burned alive in order to be purified, not literally pouring salt on one another.

Acquired Insight

2 Kings 21:6 And he made his son pass through the fire, and observed times, and used enchantments, and dealt with familiar spirits and wizards: he wrought much wickedness in the sight of the LORD, to provoke him to anger.

Observed times. What does it mean to understand time as it passes, as it is coming, seasons, eras, the signs of things to come, of what is to change, of what is to be revealed. Enchantments in the original text means to observe the signs, learn from the noted experiences, and dare to predict the future. To the ignorant, progress in thought and values and plans and creativity is the realm of familiar spirits and wizards who possess the forbidden knowledge. They speculate that these people so very different from them must have sold their souls to the devil, sacrificing babies in the forest before going to their heavy metal concert. We look back at human progress, at those who paid attention and changed the world around them, the scientists and dreamers and heretics and free thinkers, and we have to notice the shadow they always had over them of the superstitious good people who feared change and feared different.

Galileo Galilei was forced by the pope Paul V to take back that the world was round and revolved around the sun. The pope said the concept was against the Bible: 1 Chronicles 16:30 Fear before him, all the earth: the world also shall be stable, that it be not moved.

Matthew 16:2-3 He answered and said unto them, When it is evening, ye say, It will be fair weather: for the sky is red. And in the morning, It will be foul weather to day: for the sky is red and lowering. O ye hypocrites, ye can discern the face of the sky; but can ye not discern the signs of the times?

What was the sign of the times? The dawning of the age of Pisces? There are important aspects of the Jesus story that cannot be properly understood without the keys of astrological references.

Sacred Spaces

In the Bacchae, it is observed: And there through the appointed hour they made their prayer and worship of the wand. Then, Euripides imagines, every wild animal on the mountain joined them and worshipped and knelt and ramped and gloried. The wand of Dionysus, the ivied javelin, is like the image of Baal reaching down with his staff. The call to reach up and touch the staff of the god is a key to the rites of the Mysteries. Bacchus means wand, and another name for Dionysus is Bacchus.

The Bacchae references green and clustered vines to decorate the sanctuary of the tomb of the mother. This may explain the sacred groves of ancient Palestine devoted to a goddess linked with Baal.

In the Bacchae, it is sung: Wild ivy crown thy towers; oh, burst in blood of wreathing bryony, berries and leaves and flowers; uplift the dark divine wand.

From 2 Kings 23:5 we learn the priests of Baal were ordained by the kings of Judah and set up a network of sacred high places throughout Judah and near Jerusalem. In these sacred mountain retreats, they burned incense for Baal and contemplated the sun, the moon, the zodiac, and all of the stars of the night sky. All of these high places for incense, to recognize the arrival of the sun, were sanction by King Solomon the wise, the son of David. Jesus, by being called the offspring of David, is linked to Solomon's great work in promoting gnosis of the gods related to light, the myth of the scattering and reuniting of light with the arriving dawn.

From 2 Kings 23:14 we continue to explore that there must have been beautiful sacred places with images, probably depicting the sun, moon, and zodiac of stars. We can imagine incense filled the air, like the sacred frankincense that was a gift to baby Jesus (Matthew 2:11) . We can imagine groves of beautiful trees were planted around the sacred site, decorated with hand woven tapestries. These belonged to the bad guys, the lost, the not saved, the damned to hell, pagan hippies.

Rooftop Portals | Upper Room

Jeremiah 32:29 gives a window into those who prepared the roofs of their houses for the offering of incense to Baal, to look for the Morning Star, to watch the sunrise, to celebrate with drinks the "other god". These were not people standing on their roofs killing their children. These were people who so identified with the spirituality of the high places, the groves of Asherah, that they established a sacred place in their homes. For the Jews, sacred meant going to the temple, letting the priests there define the holy. What this is hinting at is the "priesthood of believers" concept. All are holy. Home altar. Home connection. Spiritual Gnostics who didn't attend the official church.

Magdalene means tower, which brings to mind the rooftop sanctuaries. It could be further explored how Baal and Asherah work as a couple, as a divine syzygy. Throughout the ancient sacred texts the two dance with different names and faces, Logos and Sophia, Love and Wisdom. One legendary early Christian Gnostic was Simon Magus who travelled with his counterpart, Helen, and as a pair they were thought to represent the ultimate Gnosis. It could be that Jesus and Mary Magdalene were once thought of in the same way, the god planting his stake in the sky while the goddess awaits in her upper room, ready to anoint the god as he arrives.

If you are on the roof of your house, don't go down to take away any of your stuff (Matthew 24:17; Mark 13:15; Luke 17:31). The remnant of Baal is to be cut off by Yaldabaoth, the rooftop stargazers (Zephaniah 1:4-5). Peter went on the roof of the house to pray (Acts 10:9). What if the very "upper room" prepared for the "last supper" tradition could actually have been on a roof?

Proverbs 9:1-6 Wisdom (CHoKMaH, Sophia) hath builded her house, she hath hewn out her seven pillars: She hath killed her beasts; she hath mingled her wine; she hath also furnished her table. She hath sent forth her maidens: she crieth upon the highest places of the city, Whoso is simple, let him turn in hither: as for him that wanteth understanding, she saith to him, Come, eat of my bread, and drink of the wine which I have mingled. Forsake the foolish, and live; and go in the way of understanding (BiYNaH). Wisdom to understanding, CHoKMaH to BiYNaH, is an amazing key to students of Kabbalah, a very private path, personal. The secluded from the world "upper room" provides only for a limited audience. The many are in need of Wisdom, but they are not ready for it. It is reserved for only the few that were present. It is up to them to partake and then to share with those they find worthy to invite to their own private upper rooms.

Mark 14:15-16 And he will shew you a large upper room furnished and prepared: there make ready for us. And his disciples went forth, and came into the city, and found as he had said unto them: and they made ready the passover.

Idols and Welcome Mats

The statues were a sign of a Baal-friendly house (2 Chronicles 28:2). The art work of the heavens was carved out of wood (2 Chronicles 33:3) or formed with molten metal (2 Chronicles 34:4).

There are very old wood carvings in Saint Sabina Church in Rome (http://rome101.com/Topics/Christian/Sabina/), one of which shows Christ ascended over and beyond the cosmos with its sun and moon and stars. Two disciples are holding an object over Mary's head and it appears she is looking up through the object to see a vision of Jesus, awaiting his Parousia.

Ancient traditions say that the Pythagoreans used a five pointed star as a symbol known by others in their secret society. Early Christians are said to have used the sign of the fish.

Mark 6:8-10 And commanded them that they should take nothing for their journey, save a staff only; no scrip, no bread, no money in their purse: But be shod with sandals; and not put on two coats. And he said unto them, In what place soever ye enter into an house, there abide till ye depart from that place.

Stay "in network" is the obvious meaning here. Show up at a house that will receive you as you arrive with only your walking stick and the shoes on your feet. No luggage. No snacks. No money in your pocket. No spare clothes. Just you and your walking stick and you are welcomed and taken care of for as long as you wish to stay in that area. I wonder what was the symbol to know which exact house to pick in an entire village?

When a part of this Essene brotherhood, the traveler needed absolutely nothing, as all needs will be provided for by the hosts in each of the villages. The guest would be fed, given a place to stay, and given items needed, such as replacement sandals. Then the guest would be welcome to speak. Perhaps the catch is that the guest must have been admitted and accepted by the Essenes, having adopted the habits and mannerisms, speech and dress. This would mean that Jesus gained disciples from the Essenes to send out as missionaries to the other Essene societies. That the Essenes had an impact on the formation of Christianity can no longer be ignored, even to the realization that a large percentage of early Christians were Essenes. Or it means the Roman writers of the Gospel stories found a Jewish tradition they could admire as they were seeking to counter the violent Zealot faction. The disciples were made up of reformed violent types, Simon the Zealot (Zelotes: Luke 6:15), Judas Sicarii (Iscariot: Luke 6:16) and the sons of thunder (Boanerges: Mark 3:17). In a sense of Roman idealism, they were all now peacefully following Jesus, the "love your enemies" non-violent Buddha for the Western world.

The Essenes are a mysterious group of Jews. They are mentioned by Josephus and Philo, but their name is not mentioned anywhere in any of the New Testament writings. Some have speculated that the Essenes were the Jews of the Dead Sea Scrolls. It is an interesting observation that Jesus is called Isa in Arabic, which could be written as Essa. This would make the name Essene to mean the followers of Essa. The references to Essenes by Josephus and Philo, two writers from the first century CE, could be to an early form of Christianity, or Jesusianity, a Jewish counter-culture that was not driving the terrorism and the war effort, but was, rather, an alternative of peace and cosmopolitan love.

Josephus: The Wars of the Jews, Book 2, Chapter 8, Paragraph 4 (78 AD): They have no one certain city, but many of them dwell in every city; and if any of their sect come from other places, what they have lies open for them, just as if it were their own; and they go in to such as they never knew before, as if they had been ever so long acquainted with them. For which reason they carry nothing at all with them when they travel into remote parts, though still they take their weapons with them, for fear of thieves. Accordingly, there is, in every city where they live, one appointed particularly to take care of strangers, and to provide garments and other necessaries for them. But the habit and management of their bodies is such as children use who are in fear of their masters [modest to avoid rape]. Nor do they allow of the change of shoes till they be first torn to pieces, or worn out by time. Nor do they either buy or sell any thing to one another; but every one of them gives what he has to him that wants it, and receives from him again in lieu of it what may be convenient for himself; and although there be no requital made, they are fully allowed to take what they want of whomsoever they please.

Acts 2:44-45 And all that believed were together, and had all things common; and sold their possessions and goods, and parted them to all men, as every man had need.

Philo of Alexandria: Hypothetica— Multitudes of his disciples has the lawgiver trained for the life of fellowship. These people are called Essenes, a name awarded to them doubtless in recognition of their holiness. They live in many cities of Judaea and in many villages and grouped in great societies of many members.

Josephus: The Wars of the Jews, Book 2, Chapter 8, Paragraph 5 in part: ...and if there be any strangers there, they sit down with them. Nor is there ever any clamor or disturbance to pollute their house, but they give every one leave to speak in their turn; which silence thus kept in their house appears to foreigners like some tremendous mystery; the cause of which is that perpetual sobriety they exercise, and the same settled measure of meat and drink that is allotted them, and that such as is abundantly sufficient for them.

This became the formula for monastic orders where wandering monks went from monastery to monastery while maintaining their personal vow of poverty.

Beelzebub Possessed House

Matthew 10:24-27 is an interesting passage that jumps to life through this lens. It is about bringing back the personal sacred space, taking back control of spiritual progress, connecting directly to the power at hand. The disciple never transcends the teacher. The servant never transcends the master.

If the house is dedicated to Beelzebub then the people living there belong to Beelzebub.

Show no fear. Everything obscured will be disclosed. Everything secret will come to gnosis. Gnosis is to attain knowledge by being perceptive, by participating, a very Zen concept. I speak in darkness about what you must speak in the light of day. I whisper in your ear that which you must go up onto your rooftops and discuss.

Beelzebub Defeats Demons

It is very interesting that Jesus never denies being on the side of Beelzebub. He questions the Jewish religion in response. If we look through the lens of "Beelzebub is not evil" then Matthew 12:21-28 (with parallels of Mark 3:22-26 and Luke 11:14-20) reads in a very different light from what we would expect.

He is the hope of the pagans. The word in Greek is ethnos, the ethnic, those outside of the band of "civilized" culture.

The Messiah was supposed to be for the chosen people, but here Jesus is presented for the unchosen outsiders.

The problem was thought to be those different, the outsiders, and the solution was to defeat the foreigners. If only Simon bar Kokhba could defeat Hadrian, the glorious new Israel would be established for the chosen people in their chosen land. It is us against them, children of light against children of darkness, angels fighting demons, good fighting evil, saved fighting damned. But Jesus is the hope of "them" more so than of "us". The paradigm shift is difficult to detect without our magic Baal lens to look through.

What if celebrating diversity is more important than maintaining sameness?

What if we stand back and appreciate life and human interaction and values and compassion on a scale beyond that of just one ancient primitive tribe?

A possessed man was brought who could not see and could not talk.

Jesus healed him to where he could then see and could then speak. The Pharisees (Jews, Fundamentalists) recognized the influence of Beelzebub in the healing miracle event.

Jesus replied that same does not defeat same. If Beelzebub is "evil" and being possessed is "evil" and evil defeats evil, wouldn't then evil cease to exist? It was a puzzle of logic that would require them to paradigm shift to answer the question. Jesus presents the logic: By Beelzebub I defeated the demon possessing the man. This is by the true god's spirit and you have witnessed its influence. The unspoken conclusion: Beelzebub (Baal) is not evil. Beelzebub is the true god. You can't see this through the Sunday school lens they provided you with. The thought is unthinkable in their paradigm.

The possessed man was symbolic of being blinded by the Yaldabaoth religion, silenced by fear. Once he could see clearly and speak freely, what would he say? Whatever he said reminded the Jews of Beelzebub, the silenced voice. After Jesus healed him, he spoke like a pagan. He was contacted by Jesus, touched by Jesus, healed by Jesus, and what did that inspire him to think, to know, to speak? The people were reminded of the legend of the son of David, of Solomon the wise. Why did the Jews not welcome the healing of the possessed man? Why did they prefer the people to remain blind and silent? In the writings of Josephus, the Jewish zealots were stereotyped as being possessed, rallying support for revolution and violence and destruction in their fanatical hatred of Roman rule. What if "violent xenophobic hate" was the demon that was cast out? This would make Jesus a "damn hippie traitor", unpatriotic to the war effort.

One with Father

Solomon's porch became a sacred place for the disciples of Jesus (Acts 3:11; Acts 5:12) according to one tradition. Jesus walked into the temple in Solomon's portico, a covered colonnade in the eastern part of the temple, the sole part of the original temple of Solomon, all the rest of which had been destroyed by the Babylonians (John 10:23). This porch was an antique treasure, finally demolished by the Romans in 70 when they came to suppress the Jewish Zealot terrorists. It was a setting that provided the scene for the question of John 10:24: are you the Christ, the Messiah? If you could go back in time and meet Jesus, what a fascinating question to ask! Is it true? Are you who they are going to say you are? His answer, John 10:30, was that he was one with his father. This is not in answer to the question. Being "one with father god" (Zeus Pater, Jupiter) was not an attribute of the Christ (Messiah).

Jupiter and not Mars? Zeus and not Ares? Whichever flock Jesus thought of himself as belonging to, he considered it to not be that of the Jews (John 10:26), to not be the Jewish Messiah. How much of his "god above god" could be edited out, explained away, drowned by dogmatic assertions and blind faith in the house of cards construction of the Bible as a continuous flowing from Jewish scripture to Gospel and Epistle traditions?

John 8:42 has Jesus inform the Jews: If God had you in his family you would have to love me. It is really about Fundamentalists of any faith. If the "God" of any people, the ongoing concept of God, the theology, the organized dogmatic assertion, cannot love the very idea of Love, then that "God" is not the "God of Love" Father of Jesus. Their religion actually blocks them from reaching out to the God of Love. They judge and hate and condemn and persecute and draw lines between people. They think they are the only ones who are right and everyone else is wrong. It wasn't just that Jesus had connected to their God in a special way. It was that Jesus exposed their hypocrisy, their blind faith in their invented projection of God, which was an idol that was preventing them from directly connecting to the Real God.

None of this is about being for or against God. It is about being for or against human concepts of God. It is about "God" being bigger than Bronze Age concepts of violent nomadic tribes. It is about "God" being bigger than one specific human tradition. It is about being for or against human imagination visions and dreams and blind faith. It is understanding that their imagined "God Almighty" is actually blocking them from relating to the actual God of Love.

Two Choices: Greed and Love

Revelation 13:9 If any man have an ear, let him hear. He that leadeth into captivity shall go into captivity: he that killeth with the sword must be killed with the sword. Here is the patience and the faith of the saints.

AL MA'IDAH 5.16 Wherewith Allah guideth all who seek His good pleasure to ways of peace and safety, and leadeth them out of darkness, by His will, unto the light – guideth them to a path that is straight.

Matthew 7:13-14 Enter ye in at the strait gate: for wide is the gate, and broad is the way, that leadeth to destruction, and many there be which go in thereat: Because strait is the gate, and narrow is the way, which leadeth unto life, and few there be that find it.

The modern buzzword of modern Christianity is faith. You can have a great deal of faith in the wrong thing. Faith is giving up on thinking and discussing and arguing. Faith is relaxing into an unquestioned acceptance. There was a lot of faith in the time of Jesus. The faith was in that their "God of victory" is on their side and that if they only stood up against the Romans that the Messiah would appear and would fight with them.

James 2.20 But wilt thou know, O vain man, that faith without works is dead?

The ancient buzzword of early Christianity is gnosis, the knowing from having directly experienced. In music, instruments resonate with the same notes. It is gnosis, obvious gnosis, when you encounter "religious" people who don't operate out of the Agape (Love) of God (John 5:42). They want to save you, change you, judge you, convert you, or after noticing that you refuse to change, they want to harass you, make you the problem, make you the bad guy.

There are two paths you can go by, but in the long run, there's still time to change the road you're on, sang Robert Plant. You have to choose what your ultimate driving force is going to be (Matthew 6:24; Luke 16:13). You either work for God or you work for wealth. The two are in conflict of interest. Greed is the cure for Love. Love is the cure for Greed. Any concept of God that promises you conquest and riches and a promised land is not of the real God of Love. That road/gate of Zealot faith will get a lot of people killed. The narrow alternative of unlearning the blind faith in the Messiah to come will let the few that take this option survive the upcoming battles.

"Pharisees" is the name of a popular Jewish sect in the Second Century. They represent "Fundamentalist" religion in the Gospel texts. Today's equivalent would be to say the "Christian Right" or the "Tea Party". Luke 11:42 has Jesus criticizing them for getting lost in the minute details and forgetting what is really important to never forget to do. This is a crisis situation. The Greek word "crisis" is translated as judgment, but that softens the meaning here. The only solution for the current crisis is to apply the Agape (Love) of God.

Get out of the details, the books and meetings and songs and sacraments, and open your eyes to what needs to be done, what needs to be changed, what needs to be fixed. Face the crisis with concern, passion, empathy, charity, helpfulness, heart.

Agape God (Luke 10:27; Mark 12:30; Matthew 22:37) with every beat of your heart, with every breath of your soul, with all the strength you have, with all you think and feel, and with every encounter you experience. Jesus proposed this be the new religion for everyone. The sooner it is adopted, the less suffering there will be in the future.

Multiplied Eightfold

Matthew 12:42-45; Luke 11:31 The ancient queen of the south travelled far to hear Solomon. Jesus is greater than Solomon. The forbidden spirit was outcast, trying to find a home in the desert, returning home he found idleness, emptiness, and only pretense of spiritual maturity. No action. No content, only hypocrisy. The forbidden spirit is multiplied, returning eightfold. They possess and influence to a much greater degree than before. Jesus was Solomon warped, the forbidden spirit, empowered, reborn, alive and active in a new generation.

Vineyard Workers

Solomon had a vineyard of Baal that he let out to keepers, each of which was to produce a profit of 1000 pieces of silver (Song of Solomon 8:11).

Matthew 20:1 For the kingdom of heaven is like unto a man that is an householder, which went out early in the morning to hire labourers into his vineyard.

Matthew 21:28-31 But what think ye? A certain man had two sons; and he came to the first, and said, Son, go work to day in my vineyard. He answered and said, I will not: but afterward he repented, and went. And he came to the second, and said likewise. And he answered and said, I go, sir: and went not. Whether of them twain did the will of his father? They say unto him, The first. Jesus saith unto them, Verily I say unto you, that the publicans and the harlots go into the kingdom of God before you.

Publicans means renters, the enterprising hard workers that were looked down upon by the self-righteous snobs, by the elite of the chosen people. This parable is very sharp pointed, stating that these outsiders, foreigners, had managed to participate in a sacred work that was not appreciated by the "good people" and these "bad people" along with their ritually unclean foreign wives (Bible code word: harlots) have found a route into heaven that is blocked for those who think they don't have to work for it.

James 2:17 Even so faith, if it hath not works, is dead, being alone.

Aten (Exclusive Monotheism)

Around 1350 BC (over 3360 year ago), a king began his reign in the New Kingdom of ancient Egypt called Amenhotep IV. In the ninth year of his being king he had a "born again" spiritual experience with a connection with a new god, Aten. He changed his name to Akhenaten. To him, Aten was not just another "god option" in a polytheistic array of choices. Aten was the one and only true supreme God and all the other gods were fake. Akhenaten thought of himself as the only son of Aten, the mediator between the only true God and humanity. It is interesting that this is exactly how Jesus came to be thought of. His Great Hymn of the Aten is very similar to Psalms 104. His Aten was Yaldabaoth before Judaism, the "no other gods before me" God to end all gods.

After Akhenaten, there is archeological evidence that the Egyptians rejected his exclusive monotheism, destroyed his buildings and art. They saw something evil in his exclusivism and intolerance of other traditions. If we tie this countering to Aten to the "exodus" of the Israelites from Egypt during the reign of Ramesses II, this would make Moses a priest of Aten, the exclusive monotheistic religion in exile from Egypt. The concept of one God along with the destruction and elimination of references to other gods returned to Egypt with the advent of Islam, with the one God now being called Allah.

With the invasion of Palestine, the one God people, led by Joshua (Jesus in Greek), forced their exclusive monotheism on the area. The existing traditions of the area were various forms of Baal and Ashtoreth, god and goddess, lord and lady. They were separate local gods but in a way they were all the same, like how it is the same "Jesus" across Presbyterian, Baptist, Methodist, Catholic, and Anglican differences.

This sets the stage for the "One and Only God" of the surviving Jewish tradition, YHWH, Yahweh, Jehovah, Yaldabaoth, in an eternal grudge match against all competitors. The result of this mindset being introduced has been various holy wars, crusades, inquisitions, witch hunts, and the ongoing manifest destiny of the replacing of all "heathen" ideas with the one "true" idea. Large boxes for narrow minds.

Zero Tolerance

Yaldabaoth turns the mountains (wilderness land of Baal) into weeping and wailing (Jeremiah 9:10-16). Baal was a religion for the "pagans", country folk, not of the civilized (lots of important words) city religion. The Baal people had followed their own imagination and in their hearts revived the dedication to Baal that they inherited from their ancestors.

Are these histories or are they fiction? In either case they inspire hatred and intolerance in the name of God to this day and unfortunately beyond. When people hold a Bible and say that it is the answer and hope for the world, I fear and wonder which parts they have been reading.

The arch-nemesis of Yaldabaoth had to be exterminated if the theocracy of his Law is to maintain control over the people. They wanted to "cut off the remnant of Baal" (Zephaniah 1:4). This set the wake into motion for the persecution of the Gnostics, the Cathars, the Gypsies, alchemy and science, witchcraft. The "homogenize and eliminate" directive from this ancient tribal religion is still rippling to this day. Destroyed in the path were the holy people, the sacred places, the relics, the sacred texts, the memories, the remnant. In every case when orthodox censorship rules a dark age is sure to follow.

Yaldabaoth showed zero tolerance. The people devoted to Baal and Asherah were violently persecuted, their houses broken down, the men charged with being homosexual and the women charged with weaving forbidden naughty tapestries for the sacred groves (2 Kings 23:7). From Geba to Beersheba, the sacred sites were sought out and destroyed (2 Kings 23:8) including the sacred left hand gate of Joshua (Jesus) the governor.

The Bacchae mentions the maids from "loom and weaving" by the magic of his breath borne away.

Matthew 5:11-12 Blessed are ye, when men shall revile you, and persecute you, and shall say all manner of evil against you falsely, for my sake. Rejoice, and be exceeding glad: for great is your reward in heaven: for so persecuted they the prophets which were before you.

Which prophets were persecuted? Why does Jesus link people being persecuted by the Jewish high priests of his day with ancient prophets being persecuted? The Zealots who had taken Jerusalem in 66 would murder anyone who did not support their cause, anyone who wanted peace, and anyone who just wanted to leave the area.

Josephus: The Antiquities of the Jews, Book 18, Chapter 4, Paragraph 1 in part: He bade them get together upon Mount Gerizim, which is by them looked upon as the most holy of all mountains, and assured them that, when they were come thither, he would show them those sacred vessels which were laid under that place, because Moses put them there.

The quest for the Holy Grail is opposed by the religion (Caiaphas) and politics (Pilate) in place. If you find the Holy Grail, you automatically win the game and you no longer need any of them anymore.

Jeremiah 7:9 asks: Will you steal, murder, commit adultery and swear falsely – and burn incense to Baal?

As if being a devotee to the sunrise was yet one more atrocity to list to the charges of the "bad people" who dared to explore a different spiritual path than the "good people" allowed. Actually it was the devotees to Yaldabaoth that destroyed property, killed people, and thoroughly misrepresented people in their self-righteous xenophobia.

If you detect any foreigners among you, kill all the boys, kill all the women who have slept with a man, but you can keep all the virgin girls for yourselves (Numbers 31:17-18).

If might makes right, and might proves which god (or rather, "concept" of god) is superior, it was Yaldabaoth that gave the chosen people their promised land through their faith and resulting actions of taking over town after town, destroying, stealing, and killing everyone except for whatever virgin girls they wished to keep. What if the Bible is propaganda and the good guys are actually the bad guys and the bad guys are actually the good guys? Hold up the traditional lens and you see it all one way. Hold up the "thought to have been destroyed" Gnostic lens and you see it all in quite a different light.

The ancient Catholics identified with the Jewish scriptures and their "council of men in charge" approved, limited and edited down New Testament. Modern Protestants identify with the Catholic Bible. Ancient Gnostics would not conceive of a Jesus that stood as an appendix to Jewish tradition. If anything, Jesus was the antidote for the violently poisoned minds of the Zealots who stood up against the Roman Empire and expected God to send the Messiah hero to their defense.

Swear falsely. What is a lie? What propaganda did they use to influence the "good people" to violently attack? It is not frankincense they are burning on the hills! They are burning babies! They are satanic death metal mockers at our family values! Exterminate. Exterminate.

Yaldabaoth has disagreeable malignant unpleasant nasty evil plans for Israel and Judah because he is extremely angry about all the incense being burned for Baal (Jeremiah 11:17). Jeremiah 12:16-17 gives the ultimatum: the people must swear to be devoted to Yaldabaoth and swear to abandon devotion to Baal or he will make the whole nation of Israel to be utterly plucked up and destroyed.

This brings up a thought. It wasn't that the Jewish people rejected Jesus and as punishment they are killed and exiled, as is understood by the Catholic fathers. It was that some believed in Jesus, were in the process of reviving the ancient religion and it was for this forbidden heresy that Yaldabaoth punishes them by having them killed and exiled. Just a thought. If Roman writers were looking for an escape clause to the contract of the Jewish scriptures, this was it. Enter the hero with the forbidden knowledge that invoked the wrath of the Jerusalem temple god and provoked it all to go into self-destruct mode.

Thomas 47 Jesus said, "It is impossible for a man to mount two horses or to stretch two bows. And it is impossible for a servant to serve two masters; otherwise, he will honor the one and treat the other contemptuously. No man drinks old wine and immediately desires to drink new wine. And new wine is not put into old wineskins, lest they burst; nor is old wine put into a new wineskin, lest it spoil it. An old patch is not sewn into a new garment, because a tear would result"

Old is Baal. New is Yaldabaoth. Incompatible world views, mutually exclusive, you have to choose one or the other. The Jewish people had a diverse history with multiple traditions, multiple concepts of God and goodness. At some point the Yaldabaoth cult emerged and its supporters wanted all other traditions eliminated. This way support could be rallied for the Maccabees, for the Zealots, for Simon bar Kokhba.

Horses were supplied by the kings of Judah to pull "chariots of the sun" as part of the Baal religion (2 Kings 23:11). Whose horse do you ride? Who is your god? Whose wine do you drink? Whose thoughts do you think? Whose uniform do you wear? Are you one of us or one of them?

There was no counter-ultimatum from the devotees to Baal. I would imagine that the Baal and Asherah people were not out to argue about the Law of Yaldabaoth. They did not consider their gods to be in competition to "The Wars of the Jews" god. They gathered, not in some defiance of the official state religion, but in pagan celebration of spiritual experience and connection. Not focused upon attacking and arguing about the Law, they were of the mindset to retire it, make it obsolete, reduced to absurdity and abandoned, left to senile old people to remember and to quote.

Matthew 23:34 reads as a summary of the persecution of the Baal prophets. From the traditional lens, it makes no sense that Jesus is saying to the leading supporters of the then modern Judaism that they represent people that in ancient times were violent towards the true prophets of Judaism. But through the Baal lens, when we consider that the leading supporters of the then modern Judaism were linked to the ancient representatives of Judaism that were violent towards the true prophets of Baal, the words take on a rich response to the most controversial thread in the Bible. If Jesus is taking a hard stance against silly rules in the Law, a hard stance against the dreamed global violence of the Prophets, and an Anti-Messianic stance against xenophobia and acts of terrorism, it would be expected that he complete the set with comments about the religious zealous inspired violence against people who considered themselves to be holy prophets of Baal. Matthew 23:34 when read as a commentary on the persecution of Baal prophets: I sent to humanity these prophets (speakers of mystical knowledge) and lovers of wisdom (Sophia, CHoKMaH, Asherah), and lovers of words. You (the ancestors of the tradition you treasure) killed them with swords, staked them to trees, tortured them in their sacred places, and pursued them from site to site with violent intent. Matthew 23:35 lists "Zacharias son of Barachias" as a gloss name for a high priest that was killed beside his altar:

Josephus: The Wars of the Jews, Book 4, Chapter 5, Paragraph 4 in part: Two of the boldest of them fell upon Zacharias in the middle of the temple, and slew him; and as he fell down dead they bantered him, and said, "Thou hast also our verdict, and this will prove a more sure acquittal to thee than the other." They also threw him down out of the temple immediately into the valley beneath it.

This was in the year 64. There is this sense of Jewish pesher style of blending current events with the interpretation of ancient texts, making the commentary relevant to the time of the writing. This theme of people in charge of the accepted religion being violent towards the true spiritual greats. In an early Christian story, James the brother of Jesus was pushed off the temple roof and died in the process. See the Nag Hammadi Library text, the Second Apocalypse of James: And they decided to throw him down from the height, and they cast him down.

2 Kings 11:18 And all the people of the land went into the house of Baal, and brake it down; his altars and his images brake they in pieces thoroughly, and slew Mattan the priest of Baal before the altars. And the priest appointed officers over the house of the LORD.

It is curious that the high priest of Baal that was murdered by the Yaldabaoth terrorists was named Mattan (2 Kings 11:18; 2 Chronicles 23:17), related to the name Matthew, the name of the author of the Gospel story. Matthew verses 23:36 through 24:2 list out the history of the decline and fall of the Jewish theocratic state as the karmic debt gets repaid. Jesus wasn't being a cheerleader for Jewish tradition, the new spokes model chosen son of the Yaldabaoth religion. In year 70 the Zealot terrorists were defeated, the Jerusalem temple destroyed. In year 135 the Messiah/Christ Simon bar Kokhba was defeated, Jerusalem renamed and Jews forbidden to return to being close enough to view their once symbolic city of victory over their promised land as the chosen people. Everything about the sacred city and chosen people was thrown down, destroyed, no Yaldabaoth to help, no Messiah to arrive, and definitely no Jesus to cry about it. He seems actually happy about it. Through the traditional lens, it is a bit confusing. Through the lens of Baal, it all makes sense.

Matthew 24:3 asks the question in focus for this lens:

When is the end of the aeon?

The word is translated as world, but the question is not when the world is coming to an end. What is being sought after here is the end of the era, the aeon, the age in which a religion like that of Yaldabaoth could have so much influence, cause so much violence and enmity and hatred. How many centuries until people are beyond tribal god violence? How many centuries until there are no more divisions that limit the scope of compassion? First one will come saying he is Messiah/Christ and deceive many (Matthew 24:5). Simon bar Kokhba is who is being referred to here. I know, that makes the Gospel a story that is written after the year 135. The Dutch Radicals are proven right in that. Wait, isn't there evidence that the Gospel dates from earlier than that? Actually, there's not, just a lot of very strong blind faith, no Carbon-14 datings, no conclusive proof of anything before the end of the second century. It very well may be, but there is zero proof. This lens brings a lot into focus in a different way than we normally see these verses. A lot of violence (Matthew 24:7), a lot of death and captivity into slavery (Matthew 24:9) where the chosen people will become hated by all people because of Jesus. Hadrian has made them outcasts. Christianity has made being anti-Semitic into an expected response. If all this were a Roman plot to neuter the Judaism of its day, it would seem it worked.

The aeon of "hatred over intelligence" has to end before humanity can proceed to evolve beyond the Bronze Age: all disagreements resolved or forgotten, all enmities interrupted with good will, all greed confronted with generosity, all violent thoughts silenced by the love of peace.

Scandal, betrayal, and hatred will become the ultimate state for those remaining faithful to the religion of Yaldabaoth (Matthew

24:10). Self-ordained "prophets" who do not know will deceive many who are so determined to have faith and believe that God will give them victory over the Romans (Matthew 24:11). The Messiah will appear! We will win! Such strong faith! Resistance is futile! Exterminate the Romans! It didn't work out for them. The Roman legions were trained to kick ass and reclaim occupied territories. They were not afraid of their superstitions about the coming undefeatable Messiah war hero.

Matthew 24:12 when read through our Baal lens: People leaving behind the Law will become the new normal, like a breeze of cool love. Once you see that, you're safe. Once the good news of the spiritual kingdom reaches the whole world, the end of the Law era will have to come. The "whole world" is beyond the scope of just the chosen people. Cosmopolitan common sense puts bigotry and narrow minded values in their proper perspective.

It is the Gospel, the good news, the cure, the antidote, the final chapter of a story that needed ending. Unfortunately the later church fathers missed the whole point and in carrying around the Jewish scriptures as their Bible, they defined themselves as the new chosen people and Europe and the Americas as the new promised lands, converted by violence and controlled by money and politics. And the beat goes on.

Matthew 24:15 leaves us with the scene of Daniel's "abomination of desolation" standing in the holy place. It is time. Who is wise from reading will understand. Hadrian placed a statue in Jerusalem in the site of the old temple now destroyed. This was the sign of the end of times for the old form of Judaism, the final chapter in the ancient epic story. It is a good thing.

The aeon closes.

Samaria

A Roman writer of the anti-Messiah hero story would be drawn to Samaria as a symbolic setting.

1 Kings 16:32 mentions the House of Baal in Samaria. Jeremiah 23:13 explains how the prophets of Samaria speak for Baal. This is leading the people astray from the orthodox (straight thinking) faith. People forgot Yaldabaoth because of the dreams they share of Baal (Jeremiah 23:27).

John 4:44 For Jesus himself testified, that a prophet hath no honour in his own country.

What makes the verse in John stand out is that it is in the context of Jesus departing from Samaria. According to Josephus, Caiaphas was taken out of the office of high priest after having persecuted an unnamed holy man and his followers that were Samaritans. This occurred in the year 36 CE, just after the time when, according to legend, John the Baptist was executed. This shows that the religion of Samaria was still at odds with that of Jerusalem, enough so that the high priest went out of his way to persecute spiritual people there.

Josephus: The Antiquities of the Jews, Book 18, Chapter 4, Paragraph 3 in part: He also deprived Joseph, who was called Caiaphas, of the high priesthood. The writers of the Gospel stories could tie back to the ancient quotes to make a strong point for those who are familiar with the references.

The old Joshua was a war hero (or terrorist leader) who crossed over the Jordan into the Promised Land. Joshua (Jesus) returned with a metaphysical Jordan to cross and a "kingdom not of this world" promised land. The kingdom of the hearts cannot be defeated by weapons. Messiah Simon Bar Kokhba lay dead, but Christ Jesus was to be venerated for centuries to come, untouchable, and thus, unconquerable.

Luke 17:16 And fell down on his face at his feet, giving him thanks: and he was a Samaritan

Luke 10:33 But a certain Samaritan, as he journey, came where he was, and when he saw him, he had compassion on him.

The Good Samaritan is the most recognized parable of Jesus. It illustrates the way that people from Samaria were thought of as being the antithesis of the accepted priests. When the people needed a physician, compassion, charity, it was the Good Samaritan that came to the rescue, not the Jewish priests. The "good Samaritan" is Jesus himself.

Matthew 28:16 Then the eleven disciples went away into Galilee, into a mountain where Jesus had appointed them.

I propose that this originally read Samaria instead of Galilee. The editing of the texts to make Jesus appear to be supportive of the Jewish religion, to be the Jewish Messiah, and to be the son of Yaldabaoth, means in part of this lens we have to read a bit between the lines and into the margin notes. In any case, Jesus didn't instruct his disciples to meet him at the Jerusalem temple, showing up all back from the dead and large and in charge. He pointed them back to the mountain retreat, the focal point for his spirituality, a spirituality at odds with that of Jerusalem.

Mark 6:46 And when he had sent them away, he departed into a mountain to pray.

Matthew 8:1 When he was come down from the mountain, great multitudes followed him.

Formula

The end of Jerusalem as being the sacred place for prophets to attempt to teach humanity, only desolation remains Luke 13:33-35.

The Law and the Prophets came to a symbolic conclusion in John the Baptist (Luke 16:16-17), but that day is done. Off with his head. Now the kingdom of God is what is important to understand. You had all better scurry to quickly get on board. The sky and earth have to crumble away before they will let go of one tiny letter of the ancient Law, but it is all dissolving quickly. The times they are a changing.

Jesus is a story about being caught in between the two prevailing religious traditions of ancient Palestine. On the one hand, he is tempted to jump off the temple roof to see if Yaldabaoth would catch him (Matthew 4:5). On the other hand, he is tempted to climb to the sacred mountain peak to worship the one (Baal) who could give him the world (Matthew 4:8). In the end, James the brother of Jesus was pushed off the temple roof and died in the process. See the Nag Hammadi Library text, the Second Apocalypse of James: And they decided to throw him down from the height, and they cast him down.

His attempts to reform Judaism from within failed. The mountain stood, promising the world. Christianity died within Judaism without a lingering spark, but spread across the pagan world, taking over the West as an international religion. In the process, Jesus is beyond the paradigm of Judaism, the paradigm of what turned out to be the surviving Christian form. He is a Mystery god savior, a great Buddha teacher, a Stoic mystic, all things to all people except he was not the Jewish Messiah warrior for the chosen people. Plot twist.

Cathars

Christianity should have put a stop to all of the madness. More peace-loving people hunted down and murdered by those who thought they represented God.

Giovanni di Lugio wrote The Book of the Two Principles, the masterpiece of Cathar tradition, which presents the ultimate dualism between the alien Goodness and the relentless eternal principle of evil that is present in all controlling government mindsets on this planet. Of course, most of this amazing text is lost (meaning all copies destroyed in flames).

For the Cathars, God is Good, defined by Good, limited by Good, therefore the god of the Bible cannot be equated with this Good. That god represents iniquity, supports fornication, destruction, the plundering of innocent lives, murder, malice, division, injustice. The Cathars condemned violence, wars, massacres, crusades. They promoted the God of light and love and peace and harmony.

The Cathars saw the Catholics as continuing the madness of the Jewish Messianic Zealot tradition of xenophobia and violent oppression and organized police action against anyone who opposed them. Their paranoid fears proved correct as the crusades were formed that murdered the Cathars and destroyed their legacy.

The purpose of Christ is to have descended from the Father of the purity and goodness beyond as an angelic being to enlighten humanity and to save us from the trappings of the evil god, the god of the Bible, the god of Catholic Christianity, the Cathars explained. They were the anti-Jehovah's Witnesses.

Pope Innocent III organized the Albigensian Crusade in 1209. The Bible was consulted and provided the will of God for the good people to label the Cathars as the bad people and to treat them like the Jews treated the devotees to Baal thousands of years before. How many more times must hatred and violence in the name of God be repeated before it is seen for what it truly is?

Lucifer: Isaiah 14

Isaiah 14:12 How art thou fallen from heaven, O Lucifer, son of the morning! how art thou cut down to the ground, which didst weaken the nations!

Weaken how? Ideas take control. Ideas transcend cultures and ages and live as archetypes. Democracy, with its manifest destiny to convert the world to US standards of capitalism, is a very powerful modern idea force. Communism, with its all for one so no one can have anything special that breaks the level field of equality of all, is another very powerful modern idea force. Islam, with its division of the world between submitted to Allah and infidel, is a very powerful modern idea force. When life is seen in terms of black and white, us and them, and you have selected one ultimate direction for your own people and for the world, then any opposing idea weakens your potential.

Why is Lucifer equated to HeYLeL in the Hebrew? The Greek LXX version of this verse uses the word phosphoros, the same word used in 2 Peter 1:19, there translated as "day star". Thus Lucifer ties back in with Baal, with the ancient network of religious competition for the promoted idea that the Jewish God is the only true god and the whole planet is destined to arrive at that same conclusion.

2 Peter 1:19 We have also a more sure word of prophecy; whereunto ye do well that ye take heed, as unto a light that shineth in a dark place, until the day dawn, and the day star arise in your hearts:

Lucifer is the Roman god associated with the Morning Star, with Venus, so when St. Jerome translated Isaiah 14:12 into Latin for the Vulgate edition of the Bible, he translated HeYLeL as Lucifer.

This is from a section of Isaiah that is used in the context of jesting a fallen foreign king. Just beneath the surface, the real meaning is the epic battle of mindsets between the chosen people with their self-proclaimed ultimate God Almighty and any dared alternative religion that has any promise of being competition.

Lucifer, son of the morning, is in reference to the god of the planet Venus announcing the coming dawn of a new day, a promise of the advent of light and warmth and life and hope. Light brings reflection, illumination, exposing and criticizing what is plainly seen to be wrong. This is the original Jewish concept of Satan, as a prosecuting attorney pointing out what is wrong, the supreme Accuser. Satan is the enlightened whistle-blower, much like how Jesus is presented in the Gospel.

John 3:19 And this is the condemnation, that light is come into the world, and men loved darkness rather than light, because their deeds were evil.

Isaiah 14:1-3 For the Lord will have mercy on Jacob, and will yet choose Israel, and set them in their own land: and the strangers shall be joined with them, and they shall cleave to the house of Jacob. And the people shall take them, and bring them to their place: and the house of Israel shall possess them in the land of the Lord for servants and handmaids: and they shall take them captives, whose captives they were; and they shall rule over their oppressors. And it shall come to pass in the day that the Lord shall give thee rest from thy sorrow, and from thy fear, and from the hard bondage wherein thou wast made to serve,

There is a reoccurring theme in the Jewish scriptures. The chosen people are trapped by foreign powers and ideas and must escape and claim possession of their promised land and purify themselves of forbidden foreign ideas. Escape Egypt. Escape Babylon. Escape Assyria. Escape the control of Greece. Escape the control of Rome. Escape being captives and assert that they alone have the true religion, the true destiny of true prophecy. Anything opposing that must be labeled and slandered and opposed. Escape European witchcraft. Escape Western science. Escape the freedoms of modern civilizations. Modern Fundamentalist Christians carry the ancient torch well.

Isaiah 14:4-7 That thou shalt take up this proverb against the king of Babylon, and say, How hath the oppressor ceased! the golden city ceased! The Lord hath broken the staff of the wicked, and the sceptre of the rulers. He who smote the people in wrath with a continual stroke, he that ruled the nations in anger, is persecuted, and none hindereth. The whole earth is at rest, and is quiet: they break forth into singing.

With each diminishing of foreign forces and ideas, there is a sense of divine intervention, a faith that their God Almighty is on their side and they can resume the synergy of his protection and blessings – in their xenophobic bubble.

Isaiah 14:8 Yea, the fir trees rejoice at thee, and the cedars of Lebanon, saying, Since thou art laid down, no feller is come up against us.

John 11:50 Nor consider that it is expedient for us, that one man should die for the people, and that the whole nation perish not.

Jesus must die to save the whole nation. Why would they think this? Why was he so important? What did he represent?

Isaiah 14:9 Hell from beneath is moved for thee to meet thee at thy coming: it stirreth up the dead for thee, even all the chief ones of the earth; it hath raised up from their thrones all the kings of the nations.

Jesus is said to have descended into hell after he was crucified, as stated in the Apostle's Creed.

Matthew 27:52-53 And the graves were opened; and many bodies of the saints which slept arose, and came out of the graves after his resurrection, and went into the holy city, and appeared unto many.

Isaiah 14:10 All they shall speak and say unto thee, Art thou also become weak as we? art thou become like unto us?

He was captured, weakened, killed.

Isaiah 14:11 Thy pomp is brought down to the grave, and the noise of thy viols: the worm is spread under thee, and the worms cover thee.

He was placed in his grave.

Isaiah 14:12-14 How art thou fallen from heaven, O Lucifer, son of the morning! how art thou cut down to the ground, which didst weaken the nations! For thou hast said in thine heart, I will ascend into heaven, I will exalt my throne above the stars of God: I will sit also upon the mount of the congregation, in the sides of the north: I will ascend above the heights of the clouds; I will be like the most High.

Matthew 26:64 Jesus saith unto him, Thou hast said: nevertheless I say unto you, Hereafter shall ye see the Son of man sitting on the right hand of power, and coming in the clouds of heaven.

Sitting at the right hand of power sounds like I will ascend into heaven. Coming in the clouds of heaven sounds like ascend above the heights of the clouds. Son of man in this concept join would be equated with Lucifer, son of the morning. Traditional Christianity thinks of the descent from heaven of Lucifer as being a rejection by God, a banishment, a punishment. What if the original Gospel thought was in more of a positive light? What if the Son of man, Lucifer, descending meant the end of the Jewish religion, or more precisely, the end of the violent Messianic terrorism faction that had taken over? From a Roman perspective, the light announcing the dawn of a new era would be seen as a very good and welcome sign.

Matthew 24:30 And then shall appear the sign of the Son of man in heaven: and then shall all the tribes of the earth mourn, and they shall see the Son of man coming in the clouds of heaven with power and great glory.

All the tribes of the earth mourn sounds like a reference to weaken the nations (Isaiah 14:12).

Luke 21:27 And then shall they see the Son of man coming in a cloud with power and great glory.

John 1:51 And he saith unto him, Verily, verily, I say unto you, Hereafter ye shall see heaven open, and the angels of God ascending and descending upon the Son of man.

John 3:13 And no man hath ascended up to heaven, but he that came down from heaven, even the Son of man which is in heaven.

John 6:62 What and if ye shall see the Son of man ascend up where he was before?

John 20:17 Jesus saith unto her, Touch me not; for I am not yet ascended to my Father: but go to my brethren, and say unto them, I ascend unto my Father, and your Father; and to my God, and your God.

Isaiah 14:15 Yet thou shalt be brought down to hell, to the sides of the pit.

Jesus descended into hell according to the Apostle's Creed. What if we continue this topsy-turvy view and apply it to Isaiah chapter 14 here? The brought down to the basest level of reality managed to plug the son of man into our dimension. So what then? The devil is the savior? Absurd, right?

Isaiah 14:16-19 They that see thee shall narrowly look upon thee, and consider thee, saying, Is this the man that made the earth to tremble, that did shake kingdoms; That made the world as a wilderness, and destroyed the cities thereof; that opened not the house of his prisoners? All the kings of the nations, even all of them, lie in glory, every one in his own house. But thou art cast out of thy grave like an abominable branch, and as the raiment of those that are slain, thrust through with a sword, that go down to the stones of the pit; as a carcase trodden under feet.

Matthew 27:64 Command therefore that the sepulchre be made sure until the third day, lest his disciples come by night, and steal him away, and say unto the people, He is risen from the dead: so the last error shall be worse than the first.

Matthew 28:2-6 And, behold, there was a great earthquake: for the angel of the Lord descended from heaven, and came and rolled back the stone from the door, and sat upon it. His countenance was like lightning, and his raiment white as snow: And for fear of him the keepers did shake, and became as dead men. And the angel answered and said unto the women, Fear not ye: for I know that ye seek Jesus, which was crucified. He is not here: for he is risen, as he said. Come, see the place where the Lord lay.

Jesus defies the prophecy. The son of man is not cast out of his grave, but rather, he is risen from being dead.

Isaiah 14:20 Thou shalt not be joined with them in burial, because thou hast destroyed thy land, and slain thy people: the seed of evildoers shall never be renowned.

In a reversal of fate, the slain Light Bringer is not forgotten. He becomes the focus of a new religion.

Isaiah 14:21 Prepare slaughter for his children for the iniquity of their fathers; that they do not rise, nor possess the land, nor fill the face of the world with cities.

It was not the Light Bringer's children that suffered. It was the Jews who lost their temple, lost Jerusalem, were sent away in exile.

Luke 19:44 And shall lay thee even with the ground, and thy children within thee; and they shall not leave in thee one stone upon another; because thou knewest not the time of thy visitation.

Isaiah 14:22-27 For I will rise up against them, saith the Lord of hosts, and cut off from Babylon the name, and remnant, and son, and nephew, saith the Lord. I will also make it a possession for the bittern, and pools of water: and I will sweep it with the besom of destruction, saith the Lord of hosts. The Lord of hosts hath sworn, saying, Surely as I have thought, so shall it come to pass; and as I have purposed, so shall it stand: That I will break the Assyrian in my land, and upon my mountains tread him under foot: then shall his yoke depart from off them, and his burden depart from off their shoulders. This is the purpose that is purposed upon the whole earth:

and this is the hand that is stretched out upon all the nations. For the Lord of hosts hath purposed, and who shall disannul it? and his hand is stretched out, and who shall turn it back?

It was verses like these that inspired the Jewish rebellions against Rome, notably in the years 66 and 132. They were filled with strong faith and zeal and the idea that if only they would remain faithful and fought hard enough that their God Almighty Lord of hosts would help them to defeat Emperor Titus, to defeat Emperor Hadrian.

What if the hated son was the Answer? What if they had fought for so many generations against the very Salvation that could have stopped all the violence and pain and suffering? What if their very scriptures that pushed them into acts of terrorism also contained the antidote key?

The rejected stone is the corner stone of the building of a new age. The rejected prophets were telling the truth. The persecuted son was their only hope. Ironic symbolism at its most poetic.

Luke 10:15 And thou, Capernaum, which art exalted to heaven, shalt be thrust down to hell.

Does this equate the ancient town of Nahum with Lucifer? This is inserted as a clue to the wise. Capernaum was the hometown of Jesus (Mark 2:1; John 6:24).

Luke 10:16-19 He that heareth you heareth me; and he that despiseth you despiseth me; and he that despiseth me despiseth him that sent me. And the seventy returned again with joy, saying, Lord, even the devils are subject unto us through thy name. And he said unto them, I beheld Satan as lightning fall from heaven. Behold, I give unto you power to tread on serpents and scorpions, and over all the power of the enemy: and nothing shall by any means hurt you.

A magic so powerful that you can command devils – that you are so connected to the serpents and scorpions that they know to not bite you – that even the powers of the Almighty Enemy cannot harm you. Who is the enemy that wants to hurt people who identify with Jesus?

Luke 10:22-24 All things are delivered to me of my Father: and no man knoweth who the Son is, but the Father; and who the Father is, but the Son, and he to whom the Son will reveal him. And he turned him unto his disciples, and said privately, Blessed are the eyes which see the things that ye see: For I tell you, that many prophets and kings have desired to see those things which ye see, and have not seen them; and to hear those things which ye hear, and have not heard them.

Nobody knows the Father. Not the commonly understood God of the mainstream religion, the Father of Jesus is alien, unknown, would have to be revealed and explained. The Father is the goal of the prophets, but Jesus is not talking about Jewish prophets here. The mysterious Father sought out by the ancient persecuted prophets once again leads us back around to considering Baal.

Forty years is a very symbolic idea in Jewish scripture

Exodus 16:35 And the children of Israel did eat manna forty years, until they came to a land inhabited; they did eat manna, until they came unto the borders of the land of Canaan.

Numbers 14:33-34 And your children shall wander in the wilderness forty years, and bear your whoredoms, until your carcases be wasted in the wilderness. After the number of the days in which ye searched the land, even forty days, each day for a year, shall ye bear your iniquities, even forty years, and ye shall know my breach of promise.

Numbers 32:13 And the LORD'S anger was kindled against Israel, and he made them wander in the wilderness forty years, until all the generation, that had done evil in the sight of the LORD, was consumed.

Joshua 5:6 For the children of Israel walked forty years in the wilderness, till all the people that were men of war, which came out of Egypt, were consumed, because they obeyed not the voice of the LORD: unto whom the LORD sware that he would not shew them the land, which the LORD sware unto their fathers that he would give us, a land that floweth with milk and honey.

Judges 8:28 Thus was Midian subdued before the children of Israel, so that they lifted up their heads no more. And the country was in quietness forty years in the days of Gideon.

2 Samuel 5:4 David was thirty years old when he began to reign, and he reigned forty years.

Luke 3:23 And Jesus himself began to be about thirty years of age, being (as was supposed) the son of Joseph, which was the son of Heli.

David's thirty plus forty ended in David's death. Jesus was positioned in the Gospel story at the year 30 and add forty years and it is the year 70, the year the Jerusalem temple was destroyed, the Zealot hopes for their Messiah to help them with their revolution failed. The Gospel was written by collecting ideas from scriptures and pagan writings. We have the what and the when and the why all predefined like a script for a play.

1 Kings 11:42 And the time that Solomon reigned in Jerusalem over all Israel was forty years.

Psalms 95:10 Forty years long was I grieved with this generation, and said, It is a people that do err in their heart, and they have not known my ways:

Ezekiel 29:12 And I will make the land of Egypt desolate in the midst of the countries that are desolate, and her cities among the cities that are laid waste shall be desolate forty years: and I will scatter the Egyptians among the nations, and will disperse them through the countries.

The temple was destroyed in the year 70. Subtract exactly 40 years and that becomes the time setting for the appearance of the rejected Answer, the life of Jesus, ending in execution in the year 30. It took 40 years for the curse to ripen in the defeat of the Jewish Zealots and the destruction of the temple. What this Jesus stood for, this "prophesized to be rejected" Answer, was the very antithesis of Judaism, the antidote, the embedded virus that if allowed to come to light could only result in the utter destruction of the entire system for all who understood the Answer.

Astrology

The stars control destiny is a very ancient concept. The progression of the zodiac signs, the seasons of the sun, the phases of the moon, the positions of the wanderers (planets), Venus announcing the coming sunrise, all symbolic to the ancient mind. The story of Jesus cannot get away from him being the sun, Mary Magdalene being the moon, the Twelve Apostles being the signs of the zodiac, his arrival at the dawning of the age of Pisces, the lamb of the previous age of Ares being slain, the fish becoming the symbol of early Christianity.

A lot of modern people consider astrology to be superstitious nonsense and take no thought into studying the concepts. This ignorance becomes a blinding force causing Jesus to not be understood in the context of the original writers of the Gospel story.

Isaiah 47:13-14 Thou art wearied in the multitude of thy counsels. Let now the astrologers, the stargazers, the monthly prognosticators, stand up, and save thee from these things that shall come upon thee. Behold, they shall be as stubble; the fire shall burn them; they shall not deliver themselves from the power of the flame: there shall not be a coal to warm at, nor fire to sit before it.

The usual "exterminate" song for any who dare to claim any sort of wisdom or insight.

Numbers 24:17 I shall see him, but not now: I shall behold him, but not nigh: there shall come a Star out of Jacob, and a Sceptre shall rise out of Israel, and shall smite the corners of Moab, and destroy all the children of Sheth.

This one verse actually inspired Simon bar Kokhba, who named himself after the word for star in this verse and proclaimed that he was the Messiah arisen to smite and destroy those who stood in the way of a new an independent Jewish state in Palestine.

The sign of the star was otherwise not thought of as being supportive of general surviving consensus Judaism, but was rather linked to the spiritual movements loosely related to Baal, and by distant extension to Dionysus himself.

Amos 5:26 But ye have borne the tabernacle of your Moloch and Chiun your images, the star of your god, which ye made to yourselves.

Acts 7:43 Yea, ye took up the tabernacle of Moloch, and the star of your god Remphan, figures which ye made to worship them: and I will carry you away beyond Babylon.

2 Peter 1:19 We have also a more sure word of prophecy; whereunto ye do well that ye take heed, as unto a light that shineth in a dark place, until the day dawn, and the day star arise in your hearts:

The day star (Venus, Lucifer, Baal) arising in your hearts is linked to Jesus here, the light shining in the darkness of the edge of night that announces the coming sudden change, the dawning of a new aeon.

Job 3:9 Let the stars of the twilight thereof be dark; let it look for light, but have none; neither let it see the dawning of the day:

It is a bitter wish to deny the Morning Star her arriving sunrise. The symbolism of wishing to hold back the coming dawn is key to understanding what we are seeing through this lens.

Daniel 8:9-12 And out of one of them came forth a little horn, which waxed exceeding great, toward the south, and toward the east, and toward the pleasant land. And it waxed great, even to the host of heaven; and it cast down some of the host and of the stars to the ground, and stamped upon them. Yea, he magnified himself even to the prince of the host, and by him the daily sacrifice was taken away, and the place of his sanctuary was cast down. And an host was given him against the daily sacrifice by reason of transgression, and it cast down the truth to the ground; and it practised, and prospered.

The daily sacrifice was fueling the very life of Yaldabaoth, but the sanctuary of the Jerusalem temple was no more after the year 70. Who is this who is so important that he puts a stop to the business of running a religion fueled by an endless stream of animals being sacrificed? Who would dare? Well, the historical answer is Titus, the great warrior from Rome with his legions of soldiers. But who is the symbolic poetic answer to what force, what mindset, what power did dare to pull the plug on the Jewish god? Satan? Lucifer? Jesus.

Revelation 1:16 And he had in his right hand seven stars: and out of his mouth went a sharp twoedged sword: and his countenance was as the sun shineth in his strength.

Seven wandering stars? Mercury, Venus, Mars, Jupiter, Saturn, Uranus, Neptune. So much wisdom, not being understood, was not repeated, not preserved, not remembered.

The Rejected One

Psalms 118:19-26 Open to me the gates of righteousness: I will go into them, and I will praise the LORD: This gate of the LORD, into which the righteous shall enter. I will praise thee: for thou hast heard me, and art become my salvation. The stone which the builders refused is become the head stone of the corner. This is the LORD'S doing; it is marvellous in our eyes. This is the day which the LORD hath made; we will rejoice and be glad in it. Save now, I beseech thee, O LORD: O LORD, I beseech thee, send now prosperity. Blessed be he that cometh in the name of the LORD: we have blessed you out of the house of the LORD.

Matthew 21:9 And the multitudes that went before, and that followed, cried, saying, Hosanna to the Son of David: Blessed is he that cometh in the name of the Lord; Hosanna in the highest.

Luke 19:39-44 And some of the Pharisees from among the multitude said unto him, Master, rebuke thy disciples. And he answered and said unto them, I tell you that, if these should hold their peace, the stones would immediately cry out. And when he was come near, he beheld the city, and wept over it, saying, If thou hadst known, even thou, at least in this thy day, the things which belong unto thy peace! but now they are hid from thine eyes. For the days shall come upon thee, that thine enemies shall cast a trench about thee, and compass thee round, and keep thee in on every side, and shall lay thee even with the ground, and thy children within thee; and they shall not leave in thee one stone upon another; because thou knewest not the time of thy visitation.

The rejected stone was their only hope for salvation, the narrow gate leading to life. They couldn't see the Answer because to their brainwashed paradigm, he looked like the devil himself, the ultimate problem, the rejected one.

Women Weeping for Tammuz

Ezekiel 8:14-15 Then he brought me to the door of the gate of the LORD'S house which was toward the north; and, behold, there sat women weeping for Tammuz. Then said he unto me, Hast thou seen this, O son of man? turn thee yet again, and thou shalt see greater abominations than these.

Ezekiel 15:6-8 Therefore thus saith the Lord GOD; As the vine tree among the trees of the forest, which I have given to the fire for fuel, so will I give the inhabitants of Jerusalem. And I will set my face against them; they shall go out from one fire, and another fire shall devour them; and ye shall know that I am the LORD, when I set my face against them. And I will make the land desolate, because they have committed a trespass, saith the Lord GOD.

Hosea 10:8 The high places also of Aven, the sin of Israel, shall be destroyed: the thorn and the thistle shall come up on their altars; and they shall say to the mountains, Cover us; and to the hills, Fall on us.

Ezekiel 20:47-48 And say to the forest of the south, Hear the word of the LORD; Thus saith the Lord GOD; Behold, I will kindle a fire in thee, and it shall devour every green tree in thee, and every dry tree: the flaming flame shall not be quenched, and all faces from the south to the north shall be burned therein. And all flesh shall see that I the LORD have kindled it: it shall not be quenched.

Ezekiel 21:2-3 Son of man, set thy face toward Jerusalem, and drop thy word toward the holy places, and prophesy against the land of Israel, and say to the land of Israel, Thus saith the LORD; Behold, I am against thee, and will draw forth my sword out of his sheath, and will cut off from thee the righteous and the wicked.

Luke 23:27-31 And there followed him a great company of people, and of women, which also bewailed and lamented him. But Jesus turning unto them said, Daughters of Jerusalem, weep not for me, but weep for yourselves, and for your children. For, behold, the days are coming, in the which they shall say, Blessed are the barren, and the wombs that never bare, and the paps which never gave suck. Then shall they begin to say to the mountains, Fall on us; and to the hills, Cover us. For if they do these things in a green tree, what shall be done in the dry?

Numbered with the Transgressors

Isaiah 53:11-12 He shall see of the travail of his soul, and shall be satisfied: by his knowledge shall my righteous servant justify many; for he shall bear their iniquities. Therefore will I divide him a portion with the great, and he shall divide the spoil with the strong; because he hath poured out his soul unto death: and he was numbered with the transgressors; and he bare the sin of many, and made intercession for the transgressors.

Mark 15:25 And it was the third hour, and they crucified him.

Mark 15:28 And the scripture was fulfilled, which saith, And he was numbered with the transgressors.

This verse missing in Codex Sinaiticus, Codex Vaticanus, Codex Alexandrinus, and others, but present in most of Byzantine Lectionary, Vulgate, Syriac, Ethiopic, and others. When we see a verse that is present in some ancient versions but absent in others, we should question was it added or omitted? This is one of those keys linking Jesus back to Baal, the heretic transgressors of the mandate to allow for no other gods before Yaldabaoth.

The Forsaken One

Psalms 22:1<To the chief Musician upon Aijeleth Shahar, A Psalm of David.> My God, my God, why hast thou forsaken me? Why art thou so far from helping me, and from the words of my roaring?

The Aramaic "sabachthani" means "spared me" and not "forsaken me". The implication is that Jesus is crying out "why won't you just let me die already?" instead of "where have you gone and why have you deserted me" which is implied in the Psalms reference. John 16:32 assures that God will never at any point forsake Jesus. The "spared me" alternative makes sense with the following event of Jesus being allowed to finally die on the cross, and before any of his bones were broken.

Mark 15:34-35 And at the ninth hour Jesus cried with a loud voice, saying, Eloi, Eloi, lama sabachthani? Which is, being interpreted, My God, my God, why hast thou forsaken me? And some of them that stood by, when they heard it, said, Behold, he calleth Elias.

Elias is Elijah, the Jewish prophet who holds the world record for having personally caused the death of the most prophets of Baal. It is in ironic ignorance that the crowd thought he was praying to Elijah, the last "saint" that such a heretic spiritual free thinker would have wanted to summon.

Son of God

Wisdom of Solomon 5:1-7   Then the righteous man will stand with great confidence in the presence of those who have afflicted him, and those who make light of his labors. When they see him, they will be shaken with dreadful fear, and they will be amazed at his unexpected salvation. They will speak to one another in repentance, and in anguish of spirit they will groan, and say, "This is the man whom we once held in derision and made a byword of reproach – we fools! We thought that his life was madness and that his end was without honor. Why has he been numbered among the sons of God? And why is his lot among the saints? So it was we who strayed from the way of truth, and the light of righteousness did not shine on us, and the sun did not rise upon us. We took our fill of the paths of lawlessness and destruction, and we journeyed through trackless deserts, but the way of the Lord we have not known.

Mark 15:39 And when the centurion, which stood over against him, saw that he so cried out, and gave up the ghost, he said, Truly this man was the Son of God.

This is not spoken by a Jew. This was an insight by a Roman.

Bodies Arose | Immortality

Dead Sea Scrolls 4Q521 Frag 7 + Frag 5 2:4-8   The good shall rejoice while those destined to die will curse the coming of the Life-giving One who resurrects the dead of His people. Then we shall give thanks and relate to you the righteous acts of the Lord…And He shall open graves…

Matthew 27:52-53 And the graves were opened; and many bodies of the saints which slept arose, and came out of the graves after his resurrection, and went into the holy city, and appeared unto many.

What is this group of resurrected saints? Is this the slaughtered Baal prophets returned from their murdered state?

Wisdom of Solomon 2:23 for God created man for incorruption, and made him in the image of his own eternity,

Wisdom of Solomon 3:1-9 But the souls of the righteous are in the hand of God, and no torment will ever touch them. In the eyes of the foolish they seemed to have died, and their departure was thought to be an affliction, and their going from us to be their destruction; but they are at peace. For though in the sight of men they were punished, their hope is full of immortality. Having been disciplined a little, they will receive great good, because God tested them and found them worthy of himself; like gold in the furnace he tried them, and like a sacrificial burnt offering he accepted them. In the time of their visitation they will shine forth, and will run like sparks through the stubble. They will govern nations and rule over peoples, and the Lord will reign over them for ever. Those who trust in him will understand truth, and the faithful will abide with him in love, because grace and mercy are upon his elect, and he watches over his holy ones.

1 Enoch 103:4   The spirits of those who died in righteousness shall live and rejoice; their spirits shall not perish, nor their memorial from before the face of the Great One unto all the generations of the world. Therefore, do not worry about their humiliation.

4 Esdras 7:31-32 ...the world, which is not yet awake, shall be roused, and that which is corruptible shall perish. And the earth shall give up those who are asleep in it; and the chambers shall give up the souls which have been committed to them.

Dead Sea Scrolls 11Qpsa:4   Plea for deliverance: For in your hand is the soul of every living being; the breath of all flesh you have given."

Ascension of Enoch

Traditions had both Moses (Law) and Elijah (Prophets) ascending into the sky and never having died.

4 Esdras 14:9 for you [Moses] shall be taken up from among men, and henceforth you shall live with my Son and with those who are like you, until the times are ended.

2 Kings 2:11-12 And it came to pass, as they still went on, and talked, that, behold, there appeared a chariot of fire, and horses of fire, and parted them both asunder; and Elijah went up by a whirlwind into heaven. And Elisha saw it, and he cried, My father, my father, the chariot of Israel, and the horsemen thereof. And he saw him no more: and he took hold of his own clothes, and rent them in two pieces.

There is sense of what if you could get back to a simpler time before history and tradition corrupted the ideas. Before the prophets' visions of a Messianic Age where the chosen people could rest in the peaceful heaven on earth of all of the other nations being powerless to invade and influence, what were the dreams of the original ancestors?

Before the Law with its rules of who deserves to live and die, what were the values of the original ancestors? Three fabled ancestors of humanity came to mind, Adam, Seth, and Enoch. Myths surrounded each, and each was exalted to an idealized hero status. Adam had lived in Eden, that ideal state which has been forbidden for humanity ever since he was kicked out by God. Seth was fabled to have the wisdom of the world carved into steles, and rediscovering this ancient wisdom made one superior to the limited understanding of the Law and Prophets. As such, many early Gnostics called themselves Sethians. It was Enoch that sparked the most interest, for he was a mortal human who was transformed into an immortal angel of light called Metatron. He was the original "son of man" ascended into heaven. What is good about Enoch is that he represented a character that could stand for something more ancient and authentic than the Judaism encoded in the scriptures and controlled by the priests.

Genesis 5:23-24   And all the days of Enoch were three hundred sixty and five years: And Enoch walked with God: and he was not; for God took him.

"He was not; for God took him" could be expressed as: "He is not here; for he is risen". The number 365 would have been interpreted by some as indicating that Enoch was destined to become a sun god, which would explain the turning into fire and glowing brightly references.

Revelation 10:1   And I saw another mighty angel come down from heaven, clothed with a cloud: and a rainbow was upon his head, and his face was as it were the sun, and his feet as pillars of fire:

Wisdom of Solomon 4:10-15   There was one who pleased God and was loved by him, and while living among sinners he was taken up. He was caught up lest evil change his understanding or guile deceive his soul. For the fascination of wickedness obscures what is good, and roving desire perverts the innocent mind. Being perfected in a short time, he fulfilled long years; for his soul was pleasing to the Lord, therefore he took him quickly from the midst of wickedness. Yet the peoples saw and did not understand, nor take such a thing to heart, that God's grace and mercy are with his elect, and he watches over his holy ones.

1 Enoch 14:8   And behold I saw the clouds: And they were calling me in a vision; and the fogs were calling me; and the course of the stars and the lightnings were rushing me and causing me to desire;

and in the vision, the winds were causing me to fly and rushing me high up into heaven.

3 Enoch 48C:1 The Holy One, blessed be he, said: I made him strong, I took him, I appointed him, namely Metatron my servant, who is unique among all the denizens of the heights. I made him strong in the generations of the first man. When I saw that the men of the generation of the Flood were behaving corruptly, I came and removed my Sekinah from their midst, and I brought it up with the sound of the horn with shouting to the heights above, as it is written, God went up to the sound of horns, the Lord went up with a fanfare of trumpets.

3 Enoch 48C:2 I took him--Enoch the son of Jared, from their midst, and brought him up with the sound of the trumpet and with shouting to the height, to be my witness together with the four creatures of the chariot, to the world to come.

3 Enoch 4:5 Therefore the Holy One, blessed be he, brought me up in their lifetime, before their very eyes, to the heavenly height, to be a witness against them to future generations. And the Holy One, blessed be he, appointed me in the height as a prince and a ruler among the ministering angels.

2 Enoch 22:8-10 And the LORD said to Michael, "Go, and extract Enoch from his earthly clothing. And anoint him with my delightful oil, and put him in to the clothes of my glory." And so Michael did, just as the LORD had said to him. He anointed me and he clothed me. And the appearance of that oil is greater than the greatest light, and its ointment is like sweet dew, and its fragrance myrrh; and it is like the rays of the glittering sun. And I looked at myself, and I had become like one of his glorious ones, and there was no observable difference.

3 Enoch 15:1-2 R. Ismael said: The angel Metatron, Prince of the Divine Presence, the glory of highest heaven, said to me: When the Holy One, blessed be he, took me to serve the throne of glory, the wheels of the chariot and all the needs of the Sekinah, at once my flesh turned to flame, my sinews to blazing fire, my bones to juniper coals, my eyelashes to lightning flashes, my eyeballs to fiery torches, the hairs of my head to hot flames, all my limbs to wings of burning fire, and the substance of my body to blazing fire. On my right – those who cleave flames of fire – on my left – burning brands – round

about me swept wind, tempest, and storm; and the roar of earthquake upon earthquake was before and behind me.

3 Enoch 48C:6 I turned his flesh to fiery torches and all the bones of his body to coals of light. I made the appearance of his eyes like the appearance of lightning, and the light of his eyes like light unfailing. I caused his face to shine like the brilliant light of the sun, the brightness of his eyes like the brilliance of the throne of glory.

3 Enoch 10:4-6 Any angel and any prince who has anything to say in my presence should go before him and speak to him. Whatever he says to you in my name you must observe and do, because I have committed to him the Prince of Wisdom and the Prince of Understanding, to teach him the wisdom of those above and of those below, the wisdom of this world and of the world to come. Moreover I have put him in charge of all the stores of the palaces of Arabot, and all the treasure is that are in the heavenly heights.

3 Enoch 48C:3-4 ...I set him as a prince over all the princes, and made him a minister of the throne of glory...I committed to him wisdom and understanding, so that he should behold the secrets of heaven above and earth beneath.

3 Enoch 48C:7-8 ...I called him by my name. The lesser YHWH, Prince of the Divine Presence, knower of secrets. Every secret I have revealed to him in love, every mystery I have made know to him in uprightness. I have fixed his throne at the door of my palace, on the outside, so that he might sit and execute judgment over all my household in the height. I made every prince stand before him to receive authority from him and to do his will.

The lesser YHWH: YH-S-WH (Hosea, Joshua, Yeshua, Isa, Iesous, Jesus)

After Words

John 8:32 And ye shall know the truth, and the truth shall make you free.

Gospel of Philip 83:13-31 It is not merely cut – what is cut sprouts again – but the ax penetrates deeply until it brings up the root. Jesus pulled out the root of the whole place, while others did it only partially. As for ourselves, let each one of us dig down after the root of evil which is within one, and let one pluck it out of one's heart from the root. It will be plucked out if we recognize it. But if we are ignorant of it, it takes root in us and produces its fruit in our heart. It masters us. We are its slaves. It takes us captive, to make us do what we do not want; and what we do want we do not do. It is powerful because we have not recognized it. While it exists it is active. Ignorance is the mother of all evil.

The Church of Christ (as it turned out) is built upon a foundation of sand and a big wave of truth is about to hit. Once washed away, the Gnostic rock underneath appears and then we can finally get on with the building project.

They read the Odyssey in Christian schools. The kids aren't going to know. The teachers aren't going to know. They don't have the proper lens to see that Ulysses is a prototype for Jesus.

Satan is code word for accuser in ancient Judaism. Jesus is the ultimate Satan, accusing Judaism of getting it all wrong, accusing their traditions, accusing their messianic expectations, accursing their persecution of the real holy peoples, and accusing their narrow vision of an exclusive connection to a war god that has caused so much suffering and death. The rejected, the suffering, the dismissed, the abandoned, the forsaken, becomes the key to the next aeon.

It is in a poetic sense that these thoughts are understood, felt, contemplated, resonated with, remembered. It's all in the mind, subjective truths, paradigm shifts of ideas and ideals that make us grow up and away from the childhood religion of our distantly remembered relatives and hometowns. You can't reconnect. You can't go home again. You once pretended to fit in, but you can no longer wear that mask.

Notes

Use the internet to search. When I was young, I paused in libraries, special ordered books, searched with very limited results. Any term you don't understand, any text you wish to read for yourself, use the internet to search. This ability, so amazing for those from the past, I fear is mostly wasted by those from the future. – Gnostic Tom 2015

References: Translations

Homer (Butler: 1898)

Illiad
Odyssey

Euripides: (Murray: 1904, as included in the Harvard Classics)

The Bacchae

Bible: King James Version (1611)

1 Chronicles; 1 Corinthians; 1 John; 1 Kings; 1 Peter; 2 Corinthians; 2 Kings; 2 Peter; 2 Samuel; Acts; Amos; Daniel; Deuteronomy; Ecclesiastes ; Exodus; Ezekiel; Genesis; Hosea; Isaiah; James; Jeremiah; Job; John; Joshua; Judges; Leviticus; Luke; Mark; Matthew; Numbers; Proverbs; Psalms; Revelation; Song of Solomon; Zephaniah

Nag Hammadi Library (Gnostic texts discovered in 1945, published 1977)

Allogenes (XI,3: Wire, Turner, Wintermute)
Apocalypse of Peter (VIII,3: Brashler, Bullard)
Apocryphon of John (II,1: Wisse)
Dialogue of the Saviour (III,5: Emmel, Koester, Pagels)
Philip (II,3: Senberg)
Second Apocalypse of James (V,4: Hedrick, Parrott)
Second Treatise of the Great Seth (VII,2: Gibbons, Bullard)
Testimony of Truth (IX,3: Pearson, Giversen)
Thomas (II,2: Koester, Labbdin)

Ancient Christian Influence Texts

1 Enoch (Isaac, The Old Testament Pseudepigrapha, volume 1, Ethiopic)

2 Enoch (Andersen, The Old Testament Pseudepigrapha, volume 1, Slavonic Midrash)

3 Enoch (Alexander, The Old Testament Pseudepigrapha, volume 1, Hebrew)

4 Esdras (Metzger, The Old Testament Pseudepigrapha, volume 1, Latin)

Gospel according to the Hebrews (New Testament Apocrypha, volume 1)

Nicodemus (Lost Books of the Bible 1926 Alpha House)

Odes of Solomon (Charlesworth, The Old Testament Pseudepigrapha, volume 2)

Pistis Sophia (Hurtak, Hurtak: 1999)

Protevangelium of James (Lost Books of the Bible 1926 Alpha House)

Shepherd of Hermas Parable (Lost Books of the Bible 1926 Alpha House)

Wisdom of Solomon (Revised Standard Version Apocrypha 1957)

Later Christian Texts

Eusebius: History of the Church book 3
Jerome Commentary on the Bible: On Matthew

Dead Sea Scrolls (Wise, Abegg, Cook: 1996; discovered in 1956)

1QH (Thanksgiving Scroll)
1QS (Charter for a Jewish Sectarian Association)
4Q252 (Commentary on Genesis)
4Q285 (War of the Messiah)
4Q521 (Redemption and Resurrection)
11Qpsa 4 (Psalms Scroll)

Philo (Yonge: 1854)

Hypothetica

Flavius Josephus (Whiston: 1793)

Antiquities of the Jews
Wars of the Jews

Qur'an (Yusuf Ali: 1989)

AL A'RAF, AL BAQARAH, AAL HIJRL 'IMRAN; AL INSAN; AL ISRA, AL MA'IDAH; AL NAML, AL NISA; AL SAFFAT, AL TARIQ, TA HA

Ulysses: Master of the House

Ulysses is the Latin version of the Greek name Odysseus. He was a great king who left his home in Ithaca to fight in the Trojan War. The queen of Sparta, Helen, was being held prisoner in Troy. It was his idea to give the gift of a giant wooden horse, out of which came his soldiers. Helen was freed. Homer's story of the Odyssey tells of his journey home. In his absence many had taken over his home and sought to marry his wife. Ulysses had to return and reclaim his rightful ownership of his house. The symbolism of the wrong people controlling a house could apply to the Jerusalem temple. It was with poetic justice that the rightful owner of the house would return and overthrow the violent greedy rebels who had taken over.

Mark 13:35 Watch ye therefore: for ye know not when the master of the house cometh, at even, or at midnight, or at the cockcrowing, or in the morning:

Solomon: Son of David

1 Kings 6:2 And the house which king Solomon built for the LORD, the length thereof was threescore cubits, and the breadth thereof twenty cubits, and the height thereof thirty cubits.

King Solomon the Wise was the son of David and Bathsheba. For his father he had constructed the original Jerusalem temple for the God Almighty of the Jews, but for his mother he constructed sacred mountain groves for Baal and Asherah. Traditions about Solomon are found in Jewish books of wisdom, Islamic tales, Medieval Magic books and symbols, and modern Freemasonry.

Messiah: Christ

In Jewish scripture and tradition, the Messiah is a prophecy of a war here to conquer the world for the chosen people.

Enoch: Son of Man

In Jewish tradition, Enoch is a human who achieved perfection and transformed into an angel of light. Traditions about Enoch survive in Hebrew, Latin, Ethiopic, and Slavonic.

Dionysus: Son of God

Dionysus is the Greek god of religious ecstasy, wine, and passion. As the Bacchae play by Euripides presents him, he is this counter-culture misunderstood rejected god-man who is put on trial, but is more powerful than those who think they have control over him. It would be an easy task to relate his tradition to that of Baal, the same flowing hair and dancing with a large pole reaching the sky, surrounded by ecstatic devotees.

Lucifer: Rejected Fallen One: Anti-Christ

The Hebrew story of HeYLeL became linked with the Roman god Lucifer in Jerome's translation of the Bible into Latin. The story is of the one representing the fallen pagan world in the wake of the Messiah's victory. In ancient thought the Morning Star (the planet Venus) announces the dawning of a new age in which the old order will fade. The symbolism is in direct opposition to that of the chosen people welcoming the Messiah who will protect them from all of the other peoples of the world. In Biblical symbolism, the new age promise of Lucifer becomes meaningless once the Messiah comes and the chosen people rule the world from Jerusalem in a peace resting on the defeat or annihilation of all who could oppose them. If the Morning Star is right instead, there is no Messianic Age to come, only the dawning of a new cosmopolitan civilized world beyond the religious walls of the dark ages of divisions and control.

Index

Printed in Great Britain
by Amazon

42852420R00088